ADVANCE PRAISE FOR
THE MASTERPIECE MINDSET

"*The Masterpiece Mindset* is a must read for parents seeking to be intentional in the way they raise their children! We have three daughters and are often stressed about whether or not we are doing things right. This book was so accessible and helpful! The stories and research the authors use helped us to reconnect with our *why*, and the tools gave us tangible ideas to implement the *how*. We feel a lot more confident moving forward in some key areas of our parenting and our relationships with our girls."

Dr. Matt and Lisa Brown, Houston, Texas, Parents of Three

"Inspiring! *The Masterpiece Mindset* doesn't pretend to be a revolutionary new cure-all to the challenges of parenting. This book is powerful because it is real, authentic, and actionable for everyday parents (like me) struggling to do a little better every day. Read it. Do the exercises. *The Masterpiece Mindset* works!"

Levi Belnap, Mountain House, California, Father of Three

"This book has refined and refueled our purpose and passion for parenting. If you feel unsure, overwhelmed, or burnt out in your role as a parent, open the pages of this book for reliable advice, thoughtful reminders, and a simple-to-follow but powerful framework to help all parents develop and create their most important masterpieces. Thank you, Annabella and Dave!"

Joshua and Katie Westover, Idaho Falls, Idaho, Parents of Two

"As parents, life gets so busy, it's difficult to determine what each one of our children specifically needs for their growth and development. Annabella and Dave have simplified the parenting process by providing a roadmap with illustrative examples, encouragement, and funny personal anecdotes along the way that leave you feeling hopeful that you can shoulder the monumental task of raising happy, productive, and self-fulfilled children into competent adults."

Ikwo and Dinah Ibiam, Wesley Chapel, Florida, Parents of Four

"What a terrific book! It's a resource that every parent should have. It's full of fresh yet timeless ideas and principles. This book will help your children better understand who they can become and give you the tools as a parent to help them get there."

Lance Garvin, Highland, Utah, Father of Five

"We really enjoyed the book! We were impressed with all the research and great ideas and so many great examples. How wonderful it would be if parents everywhere put into practice all of your well-thought-out advice! Your years working on the book will be worth all the time and effort for those parents who read it and follow it."

Margaret and Nolan Archibald, Potomac, Maryland, Parents of Seven

"This inspiring book is filled with great stories and quotes that motivate us to seize defining moments with our children and grandchildren. Really a great read for all who aspire for a mindset to influence others, especially their posterity."

Steve and Mindy Sumsion, Springville, Utah, Parents of Seven

"In a sea of parenting books, blogs, and publications that focus too much on the challenges of raising a family, *The Masterpiece Mindset* is upbeat, optimistic, and motivating. It's a book that shows you how important it is to have vision and principles as you raise your kids to become the fullest expression of themselves. We love the overarching message that we have the special opportunity to empower each of our children to develop a Masterpiece Mindset. If you are a parent, this book is definitely for you!"

Julia and Chris Warren, Poway, California, Parents of Four

"Like other great books, *The Masterpiece Mindset* comes at you with an unbelievable amount of valuable, digestible parenting tips and information! My favorite chapter from the book is "Building Your Intentional Family Culture." That might sound odd to people because my wife and I don't have any kids yet, but when we do, we'll be ready with a game plan and a vision of what kind of family culture we want to create. The principles taught in this book apply to my everyday life as well as parenting. It helps me remember my *why* for doing what I do every day and reminds me to be intentional in every area of my life. It has given me a huge paradigm shift to be more intentional in pursuing all of my goals."

Nate Heriford, American Fork, Utah, Parent to Be

"If you want more help and knowledge to help your kids flourish and succeed in their lives, this is the book! It will provide you with an extraordinary yet simple parenting roadmap as well as specific tools and principles for exactly how to do it."

Katie Dahl, Santaquin, Utah, Mother of Four

THE

Masterpiece

MINDSET

THE
Masterpiece
MINDSET

EMPOWERING YOUR KIDS TO BE CONFIDENT, KIND, AND RESILIENT

DAVID B. HAGEN
AND
ANNABELLA HAGEN, LCSW

Published by Mindset Family Therapy
Mindsetfamilytherapy.com

This is a work of creative nonfiction. The events herein are portrayed to the best of the authors' memory. While all the stories in this book are true, some names and identifying details may have been changed to protect the privacy of the people involved.

First edition published in the United States of America, 2020

For information about special discounts for bulk purchases, please contact Mindset Family Therapy @ mindsetfamilytherapy@gmail.com.

ISBN 978-0-9973210-4-3

To Brad, Blake, Mick and Jeff, our four "Whiz Kids."

And to our special daughters-in-law, Katie, Emily, and Rachel, who are the mothers of our beautiful grandchildren: Taylor, Sam, Lyla, June, Makenzie, Abby, Rose, Jackson, Luke, Hailey, Victoria, and Hannah.

May each one of you live your lives with the Masterpiece Mindset and experience a lifetime of "booyah" moments!!!

CONTENTS

March 18, 2015

Editor: "Your draft is 498 pages. It's way too long; nobody will read it."

Dave: "What if it's real good?"

Editor: "It doesn't matter; you need to cut it in half."

Dave: "How long are the Harry Potter books?"

Editor: "Your book is not a Harry Potter book."

Dave: "But we have so much great stuff to share!"

Editor: "Sorry about that. You'll have to write a second book."

Dave: "Okay . . ." 🙁

WHAT IS OUR WHY?

In other words, **WHY** did we write this book?
Well, it all began with a phone call . . .

ABOUT SIX YEARS AGO, DAVE received a call from one of our sons'
friends, who asked him to lunch. Dave assumed he wanted to
discuss business because of Dave's professional background,
but when they got together, Dave was surprised. The young father had a
different topic in mind.

"I have a two-year-old son and a six-month-old daughter," the young
father began, "and I want them to turn out well, just like your kids. What
did you and your wife do to help facilitate that process?"

After thanking him for the compliment, Dave gave all the credit to me!
Then Dave laughed and said, "Oh, if you only knew about all the blood,
sweat, and tears that went into raising our kids, not to mention the mistakes we made along the way!"

His words seemed to comfort the young father, who must have been
under the delusion that it had been easy for us.

As the lunch discussion progressed, Dave came to understand that his
real question was "How did you create the inner mindset your sons have
about themselves and toward life in general?"

The two agreed to meet again after Dave had time to process the young
father's questions and discuss them with me. We started thinking about
what our parenting strategy had been in rearing our boys—the identifying ideas, key family principles, and our family culture.

Dave subsequently shared our insights with the young father, and that
conversation inspired the thought that maybe we should consider writ-
ing a book on parenting. We discussed the thousands of parenting books
already filling the shelves.

Could we really add value to the parenting universe? We decided to try.
This book is our more complete answer to that young father's questions.

We've written it specifically for parents who really care about their children's future and who embrace that parenting commitment with vision and dedication. This book is for parents looking for an overarching roadmap to follow. We are guessing that parent just might be you.

Our overarching goal with this book is to bring out the best in you as a parent so you can empower your kids to bring out the best in themselves.

Let's be honest right up front and not sugarcoat things: parenting is a real challenge.

Trust us—we get it. Our youngest son, Jeff, has faced significant physical and mental health challenges most of his life; in particular, he has battled depression and severe OCD. Our heart goes out to him and to all those who deal with similar struggles, and we are grateful for all he has taught us.

This is the book we wish we'd had sitting on our nightstand while we reared our children. Our goal is to provide you with key principles and best practices that will help you raise resilient, confident, anxiety-resistant children who become who they are capable of becoming.

We realize every family situation is different, and we thus encourage you to adapt these ideas to your unique family dynamic, whether you are a single parent, married, or parent with a partner.

Why do we feel we can take on this topic?

Annabella is a licensed psychotherapist in private practice. She also is the clinical director for Mindset Family Therapy, where she supervises seven other therapists. For more than twenty years, she has successfully worked with parents and children in resolving difficult challenges that include:

Anxiety and depression
Stress
Suicidal thoughts
Obsessive compulsive disorder (OCD)
Underachievement in school
Lack of confidence
Perfectionism
Divorce issues

Blended-family challenges
Lack of resilience
Disrespectful and uncooperative behavior

People come from great distances to consult with her, and they come only when they have a significant problem that needs to be immediately addressed. In this book, she shares knowledge gleaned from her experiences.

Yet, even with Annabella's expertise, we realized we didn't have all the answers and that we needed to do additional research. So we spent over six years interviewing seasoned parents of now-grown children, as well as parents currently in the thick of things.

We tried to cover the gamut. We interviewed single moms, single dads, parents in blended families, and two-parent families from all walks of life and economic situations.

The parents we met generally had similar goals: to raise confident, resilient, kind, emotionally stable children who find their potential in life and become the best version of themselves.

We will share some of their stories and counsel with you.

We'll also share experiences from our time in the trenches as parents. We raised four sons, who are now in their thirties. We will tell you about our mistakes and "fail" moments we experienced so that hopefully you won't make the same ones!

Please rest assured that all your hard work as a parent will be worth it. We are now enjoying the grand-parenting stage of life as we sit on the sidelines watching our sons and their wives raise our twelve grandchildren.

We will be forever grateful for the phone call from that young father looking for straightforward answers. We sincerely hope your family and generations of other families will benefit as a result.

Happy parenting,
Annabella and Dave Hagen

MICHELANGELO

Catching a Glimpse of Your Potential Masterpiece

"Every man dies, but not every man lives."
William Wallace, Braveheart

As the great sculptor Michelangelo chiseled away at the block of marble before him, a little boy came every day and watched shyly. When the figure of the *David* finally emerged from the stone, the boy asked, "How did you know he was in there?"

"I could see it in my mind," Michelangelo replied.

The perspective with which the sculptor saw that block of marble was different than what the boy saw as he watched Michelangelo work. The artist's vision of the possibilities encased within the stone allowed him to create the masterpiece that is now a world-renowned work of art.[1]

That same visionary perspective applies to you as a parent.

In our analogy for this book, **YOU** are Michelangelo!

Who and What Can Your Children Become?

Can you visualize the future potential that lies within your children? Can you see the amazing beings who live within those blocks of stone?

Just like Michelangelo, you can help chip away at the stone surrounding your children and become an important part of the sculpting process. Just as each and every one of Michelangelo's masterpieces was unique, so is each and every child.

How do we "sculpt" our children? This means as parents we create an environment in our home that empowers them to flourish, become who they are capable of becoming, and sculpt their lives into masterpieces.

Let's be clear about what we mean by "masterpiece." Our definition for this book is children who become the best version of themselves, *whatever that looks like for them individually.*

That means all children. Children who experience significant mental or physical health challenges will probably take a different path in life, and that's perfectly okay.

We have a ten-year-old granddaughter and five-year-old grandson on the autistic spectrum. They can still become the best version of themselves, whatever that ends up looking like for them. Their parents are focused on helping them find out what they CAN do rather than what they CANNOT do.

And we will continue to be their biggest cheerleaders!

One mother we interviewed shared this insightful thought with us: "You will teach them to fly, but they will not fly your flight. You will teach them to dream, but they will not dream your dream. You will teach them to live, but they will not live your life. Nevertheless, in every flight, in every dream, in every life, the print of the way you taught them will always remain."

What begins as a parent helping their children emerge from the stone turns into children creating and realizing a clear vision for their own lives. Using the sculpting tools their parents give them, they chisel, refine, and polish themselves.

You can become the parent who empowers their children to become who they are capable of becoming, and to exceed even their own expectations for themselves.

Through our interviews with myriad parents, Annabella's clinical experiences, and our own parenting journey, we have discovered that our children need one critical life skill to realize their potential: *an empowering mindset.*

Meaning, the way they see, think, and feel about themselves. Their core identity.

We call it the **Masterpiece Mindset**.

As your children come to experience their life's journey with the Masterpiece Mindset, they can truly sculpt a "masterpiece" of a life for themselves.

What Are Some Potential Benefits for Your Children?

With the Masterpiece Mindset, your children develop a vision of their future possibilities. They come to realize who they really are and who they can eventually become.

They become self-reliant, taking ownership for their lives and not making excuses when things don't go their way. They make better choices and develop positive, intentional habits.

They become dreamers and doers and enjoy the satisfaction of hard work, maximizing their potential in all areas of their lives.

These children develop supreme confidence within themselves and in their ability to make their vision for themselves a reality. They are not afraid to fail, they experience less anxiety and stress, and they become extremely resilient at bouncing back from disappointment.

They relish the challenge of doing hard things and are assertive leaders, comfortable in their own skin and resistant to negative peer pressure. They are humble and teachable.

And finally, children with the Masterpiece Mindset have a soft heart and show compassion and empathy for others. Kind and grateful for what they have, they look for ways to build up, create value for, and bring out the best in others.

With a Masterpiece Mindset, children find real joy and experience purposeful and meaningful lives.

How will you help your children liberate the masterpiece within each one of them? How will you ignite the simmering fire of self-realization that lies deep inside their minds and hearts?

How will you inspire your children to become who they are capable of becoming and develop a Masterpiece Mindset?

How can you bring out the best in yourself as a parent so you can empower your children to bring out the best in themselves?

That's what this book is all about.

You are Michelangelo and CAN empower your children to sculpt their lives into masterpieces!

Next, we will provide you with a potential parenting plan to help you make that happen.

THE VIP PLAN

"To create a masterpiece, you have to master each piece."
Craig Valentine

LET'S BE HONEST—PARENTING IS TOUGH. There are no guarantees, nor is there a one-size-fits-all parenting strategy. Why? Because every child comes wired differently and has the agency to make their own decisions.

In light of this fact, does it make sense to have an overarching plan for, arguably, the most important thing you will ever do? We think so! As you think about your children and their future potential, do you have an intentional plan to help them get there?

At age eighteen, your children will probably (maybe hopefully!) be on their way to the next chapter in their lives and leaving your home. The time of your greatest influence on their lives will be over.

Will they become who you hoped they'd become?

TODAY | WHAT'S YOUR PLAN TO GET THEM THERE? | YOUR CHILDREN'S POTENTIAL

In the next few pages, we'll introduce a potential parenting plan that can empower your children to sculpt their lives into masterpieces. Whether you are a single mom or dad, married, or parenting with a partner, this plan can benefit you.

We are not suggesting this is the *only* parenting plan that can be used to achieve your parenting objectives, but we do suggest that this is one parenting roadmap you should strongly consider.

During a vacation trip to Italy, we found exactly what we'd envisioned—a country with incredible history, unbelievably good food (gelato and pizza!), and stunning museums and art galleries. And Italy was, of course, home to Michelangelo.

He was born in the Florence area but spent significant time in Rome producing art for various patrons. Though he was an expert painter and architect, his first love was sculpture.

We were inspired as we took in many of his stunning masterpieces, including the *David*, the *Pieta*, and the ceiling of the Sistine Chapel. We became curious about his life and his genius.

How was he able to create such an extraordinary number of majestic art pieces over the course of his almost eighty-nine years? What was his mindset as he crafted his masterpieces?

Was there anything we could learn from him applicable to parenting?

We think so! What we learned from Michelangelo led us to developing our parenting plan—a parenting roadmap for creating dramatic results in the lives of your children, and leading them to developing the Masterpiece Mindset.

We call it the **VIP Plan**.

Why? Because *every parent is a VIP* (very important parent) in the lives of their children. The VIP plan looks like this:

V *Vision*

I *Intentional Family Culture*

P *Principles*

VISION

One thing we definitely learned from studying Michelangelo was that he began each of his projects with a vision of what he wanted the finished product to look like. It didn't always turn out exactly as planned, but it did give him a clear direction with which to proceed.

This same visionary approach applies to your parenting.

It's so easy to get caught up in the day-to-day hustle and bustle of homework, dance practices, sporting events, and other activities that parents sometimes forget to look at the bigger picture.

Imagine that you could look through a pair of binoculars and see far off into each of your children's future. What would you see? What could life look like for them? Who and what could they become?

Try to visualize the finish line from the starting line for each one of your children. Your vision of their potential becomes the starting point for your parenting journey and will help you parent with confidence, intention, and clear direction.

Your vision for your children becomes your **WHY** for doing the things you do every day as a parent. If your *why* is powerful enough, the *how* becomes easier.

So what is your **HOW**? How can you empower your children to develop the Masterpiece Mindset and sculpt their lives into masterpieces?

The answer lies below.

INTENTIONAL FAMILY CULTURE

Michelangelo was very intentional about the way he went about his work. Likewise, you can be intentional about the way you parent.

All thriving, successful organizations have a culture that directs and empowers their members. Google, Twitter, Southwest Airlines, Chevron, and Zappos are examples of companies known for their thriving, empowering cultures.

Thriving, successful families are no different.

Your family culture is how you think and act as a family. It is your family's unique way of doing things. It includes the key principles your family hangs its hat on.

Your family culture will trump anything else you ever do as a parent. It is where the magic happens. Every family has a culture whether they realize it or not.

The key is to make your family culture ***INTENTIONAL****.* An intentional family culture is one where you deliberately decide what you want your family culture to look like and what key principles are most important to your family.

For example, the same child could be raised in three different families, with three different family cultures, and he or she would probably turn out differently in each one.

Yes, there are those children who would challenge any parent no matter what those parents did in their home. But we believe the odds of garnering positive results with your children will be greatly enhanced when you implement an intentional family culture.

The overall objective of your intentional family culture is to turn your key family principles (this is "how **we** think and act as a family") into individual beliefs for each one of your children ("this is how **I** think and act").

Here is a simple example of one father teaching his son about a family principle:

> When my son Alex was six years old, we were on a walk, picking up garbage along the way. I asked him, "Why are we doing this? Is it to make the street look better?"
>
> He answered in the affirmative.
>
> "That's part of it," I said. "But more importantly, we do it because that's just the kind of people we are. We make things better than how we found them.
>
> It makes no difference who notices—what really matters is that we will know that we picked up garbage when we found it."[1]

Your intentional family culture is the potential masterpiece you can sculpt as a parent. It is your equivalent of Michelangelo's David.

You can sculpt an environment in your home that empowers your children to become who they are capable of becoming and develop the Masterpiece Mindset.

In this book, we will devote two full chapters to showing you how to build an empowering, intentional family culture within the walls of your home.

Building an intentional family culture in your home leads us to the final part of our parenting roadmap, which is your **WHAT**.

What specifically do you teach your children within your family culture that will give them the best chance of becoming the best version of themselves?

The answer is below.

PRINCIPLES

You intentionally teach *seven key principles* to your children.

These seven key principles are powerful, practical, and timeless.

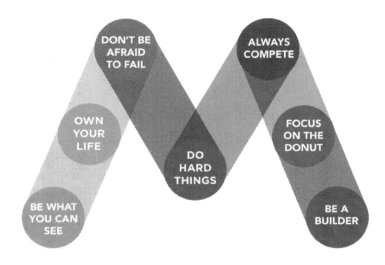

Each of the seven key principles is designed to be a "message with a heartbeat" and eventually become *deeply rooted inner beliefs* within the minds and hearts of your children. These inner beliefs become part of their *core identity* ("This is who I **AM**").

As your children internalize and begin to live their lives with these seven key principles, they will come to know who they really are, where they are going, and how to get there. That is powerful.

These seven key principles have surfaced repeatedly in our interviews with other parents and in our personal parenting journey. These foundational principles become solid anchors in the lives of your children.

We will introduce and discuss each key principle in detail in its own chapter.

No matter your specific vision for your children's potential, these seven key principles can help them get there.

With the Masterpiece Mindset, sculpting a masterpiece of a life is possible for your children.

Ten-Second Summary

The VIP Plan

V—Vision
I—Intentional Family Culture
P—Principles

OUR INVITATION

As this chapter draws to a close, we invite you to consider the following three questions. Please take a minute and jot down your answers.

1. What is your vision for your children's potential?

2. What are some of your thoughts or ideas about creating an intentional family culture in your home?

3. What do you see as potential benefits for your children as you teach them the seven key principles within your family culture?

OUR PROMISE

The VIP Plan can serve as an overarching compass and roadmap for your parenting efforts. It will bring out the best in you as a parent so you can empower your children to bring out the best in themselves. We promise you that if you do your best to fully engage in the VIP Plan, you will see dramatic results in the lives of your children.

Under your guidance, your children can become who they are capable of becoming and sculpt their lives into masterpieces, whatever that looks like for them individually.

As you engage in principle-based parenting with the VIP Plan, you will parent with more confidence, intention, and control.

Your family culture will trump anything else you will ever do as a parent. As your children internalize and live the seven key principles, they will govern themselves without your constant guidance or supervision for the rest of their lives.

They develop a powerful *core identity* ("This is who **I AM**") and the Masterpiece Mindset.

As your children come to understand who they really are, it is much easier for them to see who they can really become.

The Masterpiece Mindset can become the greatest family legacy you give to your children. Your children and future grandchildren will be forever grateful for your vision, commitment, and consistent execution of the VIP Plan.

Never forget that you will always be a **VIP** in the eyes and lives of your children!

You are Michelangelo and CAN empower your children to sculpt their lives into masterpieces!

BUILDING YOUR "INTENTIONAL" FAMILY CULTURE

*"Culture is the engine, it drives everything that happens
in an organization, every single day."*
S. Chris Edmonds

L ET'S TOUCH BASE IN ROME, where Michelangelo enjoyed many
years of immense success creating his majestic masterpieces. The
famous expression, "Rome wasn't built in a day," reminds us that
it takes time to create something special, that we need to be patient and
stay the course.

And so it will be as you build your intentional family culture.

But let's consider the rest of the story. It's true that Rome wasn't built
in a day, but one thing they did do every day was lay bricks, hour by
hour, day after day, for years and years.

It's easy to overestimate the importance of building the Roman empire,
and underestimate the importance of laying just one more brick.

It doesn't take an inordinate amount of work, or require an impressive amount of strength, skill or intelligence to lay one brick. Nobody is going to throw you a parade or put you on a magazine cover for laying a brick.

But laying bricks every single day, for years and years and years. That's impressive.

That's how the Roman empire was built, and that's how your intentional family culture will be built. Brick by brick, day by day.

As children grow, their lives typically become a reflection of their family culture. Your "intentional" family culture is your purposeful and deliberate effort to teach your children the key principles you want them to live their lives by.

Be intentional about being intentional.

Your family culture is your family imprint, your family DNA, your family identity. "This is how we [insert your family name here] do things in our family." Your family culture is the laboratory where key family principles are taught, internalized, and experienced.

Every family has a culture, either by intentional design or by default.

Don't leave your family culture to chance. Your default family culture is probably the culture you were raised in because it's what you instinctively know. That may be fine, or it may not be, depending on the specific family challenges you experienced.

If you identify some things you want to do different than your parents did, don't be afraid to make changes. Take what you like to your family culture and leave the rest behind.

If you change nothing, nothing will change.

The most important question to ask is whether your current family culture will empower your children to sculpt themselves into masterpieces by developing the Masterpiece Mindset.

For as Dr. Hilarie Cash, a renowned psychotherapist in Seattle, Washington, has said, "If the culture you are embedded in isn't healthy, you're going to end up with an unhealthy individual."

Dave used to teach a Sunday School class of fourteen- and fifteen-year-olds at our church. One day during class, he asked the young women and young men the following questions:

- What does your family name represent?
- What are three principles your family lives by?
- How would other people describe your family?

He was surprised when he initially got a lot of blank stares. The class members didn't seem to understand his questions. With a little coaching, they figured out what he was really asking, and he got some interesting responses—though most of their feedback was not very specific.

How would your children respond? It may be an interesting exercise for you to ask them. In your intentional family culture, your children can come to clearly know what your family name represents, what your key family principles are, and why they are so significant to you.

As you contemplate your current family culture, consider these questions:

- What is our current family culture teaching our children?
- What are the key principles by which our family lives?
- Is there anything we need to stop doing?
- Is there anything new we need to start doing?
- What should we keep doing so that we can achieve our desired results?

At the end of the day, your children will reap the family culture you sow. Your family culture will trump anything else you will ever do as a parent.

It's interesting how the word *culture* derives from the tilling of soil—think *cultivate*—and how powerfully it affects whatever grows in a particular place. Your family culture is your garden.

The key principles you teach and live by are the seeds you are planting within your children's minds. As your children have experiences that nourish these seeds, they grow into deeply rooted beliefs about themselves. These inner beliefs become part of their core identity.

Let's take a deeper dive into your potential intentional family culture, but before we do, let us share a few *important* parenting reminders.

Please never forget that you **DO NOT** need to be a perfect parent to garner positive results. We've never met a perfect parent, have you? It's certainly not us, and it won't be you. Do not compare yourself with other parents or your kids with other people's kids.

Comparison is the thief of joy.[1]

Always remember that you are good enough, and that you are doing better than you think you are! The road to parenting success is always under construction, so just keep going and remember why you started. Focus on your progress, not on perfection.

It is okay to be self-aware of things you may need to work on, but it's NOT okay to be self-critical of yourself. There is a significant difference.

Your parenting journey is about becoming "your" best, not "the" best. Simply try to bring out the best in yourself as a parent so you can empower your children to bring out the best in themselves.

Never forget that you are the real "superhero" in your children's lives!

How do the 7 Key Principles lead your children to develop the Masterpiece Mindset?

Here is a visual representation of your children's pathway to the Masterpiece Mindset:

7 Principles > Experiences > 7 Beliefs > The Masterpiece Mindset

Seven principles are taught to your children.
Experiences that reinforce and affirm the seven principles.
Seven beliefs resulting from the "right" kind of experiences.
THE MASTERPIECE MINDSET is the end result.

A masterpiece of a life is then possible for each of your children.

SEVEN KEY PRINCIPLES

The seven key principles are powerful, practical, and timeless and create a solid foundation for your intentional family culture. They become the guideposts your children look to for direction and inspiration. The goal is for these seven key principles to eventually become seven deeply rooted beliefs within your children's minds and hearts.

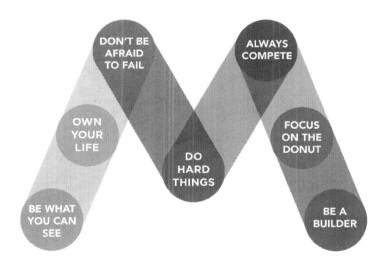

During one of our interviews, we asked one mother, "What does it mean to you to be a good parent?" This was her insightful response: "That is a big question, and one I have given much thought and reflection.

I see my role as making sure that this human I brought into the world can be the best they can be, that they are equipped with the right information and the right guiding principles.

That I'm basically like their shaman to take them until they're ready to go out on their own. It's my job to make sure that they're fully prepared for life."

The key principles you teach will seep through the walls of your home in such a powerful way that your children will feel and breathe them every day. They can become an integral part of your family identity and provide an illuminating light for your parenting journey.

You will find that the transformational power contained in the seven key principles creates a culture of empowerment, as well as a shield or protective armor when your kids are outside your home.

Repetition aids retention.

As you begin to plant the seeds of the seven key principles from a very young age, you will be amazed at how quickly they begin to take root in your children. Never underestimate the power of planting a good seed!

Your children come to know who they really are, where they are going, and how to get there. They become who they are capable of becoming.

What is rewarded is repeated.

Try to catch your children living the principles and reinforce the behavior by instantly recognizing it and celebrating it. Recognize and celebrate any behavior in alignment with the seven key principles.

EXPERIENCES

Experiences create beliefs.

No parent thinks, "I wonder what I can do today to undermine my children, subvert their efforts, turn them off learning, and limit their achievement." Of course not. They think, "I would do anything and give anything to help my children become successful."

Yet many of the things we do tend to boomerang. Our "helpful" judgments, lessons, and motivational techniques often send the wrong message.[2]

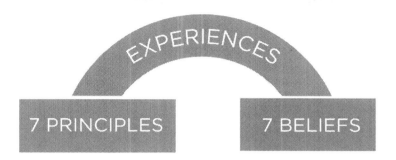

Experiences are the "bridge" between the seven key principles you are teaching and the seven beliefs you desire your children to internalize. Your children's experiences in life will lead directly to their beliefs about themselves and their core identity.

Everything about their external life is a reflection of their inner beliefs.

Learning from experience teaches your children in ways nothing else can. What is it about experience that is so essential to creating your children's inner beliefs?

They don't just learn from absorbing facts and information. Each of the seven key principles is designed to be a principle of action, understood first by definition, and then, more importantly, by *experience,* so that they really ring true in your children's minds and hearts.

Seek out experiences that reinforce and affirm the seven key principles.

One of our friends is Nolan Archibald, who became a CEO of a Fortune 500 company—Black and Decker Corporation—at age forty-two, the youngest in history to do so at the time. His journey getting there is a great illustration of the benefits of experiences.

Upon graduation from Harvard Business School, he had many job offers. Most of his classmates took jobs offering the most money or the most prestigious titles. He took a different, more intentional approach.

Archibald knew his ultimate goal was to become CEO of a Fortune 500 company. He also knew that if that were going to happen, he would need a range of job experiences within his career path to prepare him to eventually run a major international corporation.

So rather than chase dollars or titles, he focused on one issue when looking at a potential job opportunity: "Whenever I considered a new job, I made the decision solely on whether this experience would increase my probability of becoming a general manager, and subsequently a CEO of a Fortune 500 company.

Salary and title were unimportant."[3]

Consequently, Archibald's first job out of business school was running a mine in Canada. He said that experience was invaluable in his training and preparation. He ultimately was the CEO at Black and Decker for twenty-six years, and retired when he facilitated a merger between Black and Decker and the Stanley Tool Company.

He had a clear vision of his career "finish line" and mapped out the experiences (the process) he would need to get there.

You can have a similar intentional approach as a parent.

Experiences come in all shapes and sizes, both inside and outside the home. Regularly ask yourself, "What experiences can I facilitate for my children that will reinforce the seven key principles we are teaching?"

Try to spend your time and hard-earned money on experiences that provide your children with the right kind of takeaways.

Whether you realize it or not, you create experiences every day that shape the beliefs of your children. You send signals, consciously or unconsciously, that teach them how to think and act.

Each interaction with your children creates an experience that can either foster or undermine the principles you are attempting to teach.

Personal Modeling

It is better to see a sermon than hear a sermon.

One of the greatest truths we can learn in life is that the only person we really have control over is ourselves. To begin a transformation in your family culture, the change must start with you as a parent.

The power of example is the greatest power in the world. The most important experience you can provide for your children is to do your best to live your life in alignment with the seven key principles.

As a parent, you have the opportunity to model the life you want your children to live. An intentional parent is one who knows the way, goes the way, and shows the way.

You are the ultimate role model for your children. The reality is that your children will follow your example more than your advice. Kids typically model the behavior they are shown by their parents.

To become a great leader, you must first become a great learner.

As you learn, internalize, and live by the seven key principles, you will naturally become a more effective parent.

The story is told of a dog who wandered into a man's home. His three sons played with it, fed it, and soon became quite fond of it. It so happened that the dog had three white hairs in its tail.

One day, the man and his sons spotted an advertisement in their city newspaper about a lost dog. The description in the newspaper perfectly matched the stray dog they had taken in.

The man later said, "In the presence of my three boys, we carefully separated the three white hairs and removed them from the dog's tail." The real owner of the dog eventually discovered where his stray pooch had gone and came to claim him.

The dog showed every sign of recognizing his owner, and the owner was ready to take him away.

At that point, the father spoke up and asked, "Didn't you say that the dog would be known by three white hairs in his tail?" The owner, unable to find the identifying feature, was forced to admit that this dog didn't fit the description, and he left.

Years passed, and the dad sadly said, "We kept the dog, but *I lost my sons* that day."[4]

What about your children's experiences OUTSIDE your home?

This is more challenging because you obviously have less control. What type of activities should your children be engaged in? Here are a few questions to ponder as you think that through:

- Will the experience help my children develop the "right" kind of beliefs about themselves?

- Will my children enjoy and fully engage in the activity?

- Will my children receive the benefits they should from this experience?

- Will our key family principles be reinforced and affirmed?

Hopefully their extracurricular activities are teaching them the *right* lessons, meaning lessons that align with the seven key principles. Think short-term and long-term takeaways.

William was a young college student who decided to take a summer job selling pest-control services door-to-door in a state far from his home. It was a 100-percent commission job, but the potential financial rewards were substantial.

He knew it would be very hard, but he would get to work with two good friends. It appeared to be the perfect job, and he was excited at the prospect.

Unfortunately, it did not work out for him. Sales was not a good fit for his personality, and he quit after three weeks. His friends decided to stay. He came home feeling like a loser, and his confidence plummeted.

This experience had the potential to negatively affect his inner beliefs about himself, and his ability to do hard things in his life going forward.

So what could his mother do to help him process the experience in a more positive way, and hopefully make sure there were no lingering long-term negative effects?

She first acknowledged and validated his feelings. "I'm sorry it didn't work out for you. I'll bet it hurts that your friends are still selling and you came home," she said. She then let him vent a little bit and verbally process his feelings about the experience.

Next, she walked him through why the job was probably not a good fit for him from the start, and they talked about what he had learned about himself from the experience.

"At least you made the effort," the mother said, "and found out valuable information about yourself." She reminded him of the many hard things he had successfully completed in the past.

Because she handled the situation as well as she could, his beliefs about himself appeared to remain positive, and he was determined to continue to try new things that would challenge him in the future.

Your goal as a parent is to help your children create positive beliefs so deeply imbedded in their minds and hearts that they can overcome any of the negative experiences that will certainly come their way.

The messages your children receive from others can be very negative and confusing, especially during the brutal middle school and high school years.

Make sure they are receiving contrasting positive messages from you. Let your messaging to them be clear, intentional, and pure. Frame your messages in such a way that they are empowering as well as enjoyable for your children.

Role Models and Mentors

Role models can also create empowerment in the life of your children. Seek out those who will provide the right kind of example and experiences. Good role models show children what they really are capable of.

Point out role models who live in alignment with any of the seven key principles. These can include educators, grandparents, siblings, clergy, peers, and any number of ordinary people encountered in their everyday lives.

The best role models will be people your children know personally.

Sonia Sotomayor, a U.S. Supreme Court justice, said this: "A role model in the flesh is much more significant than an abstract role model. A role model in the flesh provides real inspiration and provides confirmation that it is possible."[5]

In other words, "Yes, someone like me can do this."

One father we interviewed was raised by his mother as his father was in prison for most of his younger years. He needed a male role model who could help show him the proper way to do things and let him know that he was capable of accomplishing great things in his life.

His role model came in the form of a friend's father who took him under his wing and included him in family activities, discussed life with him, and inspired him to dream big.

He said, "He saw things in me I didn't see in myself. He helped me see my potential, and I believed him. I would not be where I am today without him, plain and simple."

Young people typically choose role models based on the mindset they are developing toward realizing their own aspirations. You may want to ask your children who their role models are and why. It could lead to an interesting, fruitful discussion.

In addition, a good mentor can create real value and inspiration for your children. A few words of encouragement from the right person at the right time can change everything.

Sometimes it's better for your children to hear the same thing they hear from you from the lips of other people!

Justice Sotomayor grew up in a single-parent household with her mother. It was a difficult environment in which to develop any kind of deep confidence or vision.

She gives all the credit to her grandmother, who served as a constant mentor to her growing up—and, most importantly, gave her the courage to pursue her dreams.

She said that without her grandmother's encouragement, she would not be where she is. *"She believed in me when I did not believe in myself."*[6]

SEVEN BELIEFS

Beliefs create mindset.

Your children's inner beliefs are the lens through which they will see themselves and life in general. The way they think directly affects the way they behave. A preoccupation with your child's behavior in and of itself will not change their behavior.

If you want to change the way your children behave, you have to change the way they think. Whether they are accurate or not, we all live our lives based on our inner beliefs and core identity.

Beliefs begin to form in early childhood.

As we grow up, we all develop ideas about ourselves, others, and the world around us. These beliefs become deeply imbedded within us.

Our present is shaped by our past, and we are, in many ways, its product.

We view our beliefs as truth and these "truths" become our inner compass throughout life. Beliefs are built layer by layer, experience by experience, similar to peeling back the layers of an onion, and lead directly to your children's mindset.

As renowned Harvard psychologist William James came to believe after years of research about the human mind and behavior, "People tend to become what they think of themselves."[7]

Over time, and given the "right" kind of experiences, **the seven key principles become seven deeply rooted beliefs within your children's minds and hearts,** giving them a deeply ingrained **core identity** ("this is who **I AM**").

The combination of the seven beliefs creates the Masterpiece Mindset.

Here are the *seven beliefs:*

BELIEF 1
I AM a person who can be what I can see in my mind.

BELIEF 2
I AM the owner of my life.

BELIEF 3
I AM not afraid to fail.

BELIEF 4
I AM a person who can do hard things.

BELIEF 5
I AM a person who competes in everything I do.

BELIEF 6
I AM grateful for who I am and what I have.

BELIEF 7
I AM a builder of other people.

That is the Masterpiece Mindset!

What could life look like for your children if they develop this core identity for themselves? Could they sculpt their lives into masterpieces?

Your children will come to know who they really are. And when your children know who they really are, no one else has the power to tell them who they should be. That is an empowering life-changing mindset.

As the Masterpiece Mindset is unleashed in their lives, a masterpiece of a life is right around the corner.

As a psychotherapist, Annabella has found this to be true. She has worked with many individuals who had negative beliefs. These beliefs significantly affected their happiness, well-being, and their ability to function in a productive manner.

When a person is under stress or experiencing difficulty, the normal tendency is to default to their negative beliefs, which in turn, confirm *wrongly* what they already believe about themselves. It becomes the wrong kind of "evidence."

Quite often they don't even realize what these beliefs are. Once they uncover their specific negative beliefs, Annabella can then go to work to help them create new positive beliefs. They work together to find evidence that supports these beliefs.

This process takes time and significant effort on the individual's part, but it can be done. Ideally, you want to prevent your children from creating negative beliefs about themselves in the first place.

Think about the security system at the airport. We all wait in line for our turn to go through the scanner to make sure we're not carrying anything dangerous onto the plane. Sometimes we're even "randomly selected" for more detailed searches. Been there, done that!

Wouldn't it be nice for parents to have a "belief scanner" for their children? How wonderful would it be to have the ability to look into our children's minds and hearts and see how their experiences on any given day have affected them.

With that ability, we could help walk them through the "negative" experience again, then help them re-script and reframe it in a more positive way. Obviously, this isn't possible, so what can we do?

Consider this. We recently saw a three-year-old girl at the park point to a dog and say "Bad dog." She didn't know this particular dog, but evidently she had already formed a negative belief about dogs in general. Where did this idea come from?

Where was the "evidence" that this dog was bad? Maybe she had been bitten by a dog, or maybe someone told her that all dogs were scary and bad. Who knows? The dog was just lying down resting and did not look threatening in any way. To us, it seemed to be a "nice" dog.

At this point, it did little good to dwell on how her beliefs had been formed. The important question was how they could be changed. There needed to be some re-scripting of her ideas about dogs to create a new belief.

First off, she could be told the opposite—that dogs were good. Second, she needed to have an experience to create new "evidence" that dogs could, in fact, be good.

So what happened? Her caretaker took her over to the dog, and they spent a minute just looking at it. The dog did not react. Then the caretaker helped her to pet the dog. Again, the dog was friendly and let her pet him with no problem.

The little girl smiled, continued to pet the dog, and was now clearly comfortable.

She now had new "evidence" that dogs could be good. This one "new" positive experience, if followed by subsequent similar experiences, would lead her to develop a new, permanent inner belief about dogs.

Regularly try to monitor your children's developing inner beliefs about themselves. What are *three key indicators* that can help you track their progress?

First, your personal observance of their behavior. Any potential red flags?

Second, seek out the insights of others who interact with your children outside your home. These can be friends, teachers, coaches, or leaders etc.

Ask them questions like these:

- Have you witnessed any specific behaviors we should be concerned about?

- Is there one area you think we need to focus our efforts on right now?

- How successfully and confidently is she interacting with her peers?

Children who have a vision of who they really are, are built, not born.

Try to stay focused on your children's progress, and see them as they can *eventually* become. Their lives are about becoming, becoming who they are capable of becoming. Becoming the best version of themselves, whatever that looks like for them individually.

You can't microwave the "becoming" process. Be patient, it takes time.

And never forget that it's never too late for your children to become who they are capable of becoming.

Just because they are wandering doesn't mean they are lost. If they are struggling, be patient and double down on unconditional love. Or try a different approach.

If you change nothing, nothing will change.

In reality, there is no real health without mental health. Let's talk about the benefits of therapy for a minute.

Different circumstances may lead us or our children to attend therapy and there is nothing wrong with that. On the contrary, it can be of great benefit.

Through therapy, children and adults learn to recognize their strengths, find hope, motivation, and resilience. Therapy can provide individuals with skills and tools to address their current challenges.

Most importantly, it helps individuals to start doing what matters most in their lives and living purposefully despite the adversities that define the human experience.

Recognizing the need for therapy and acting on it is a sign of strength, not weakness. Unfortunately, too many are still misinformed in that regard.

In addition, therapy is not just for critical matters.

It can also be a vehicle to improve in different areas of our lives. Many individuals seek therapy so that they can enhance their communication, leadership, parenting, and self-compassion skills as well as other areas of their lives.

Third, schedule regular meetings with your spouse, partner, trusted friend, or relative, etc., to see how they feel your children are doing. Discuss insights and ideas about potential solutions or actionable strategies you might implement in your home.

"What is going right?" "What is not going so well?" "What can I or we do better?"

As a parent you are the most powerful teaching force for good that your children will ever have. You will have feelings and insights no one else has. Trust yourself.

THE MASTERPIECE MINDSET

The Masterpiece Mindset is a combination of the seven beliefs.

The mind is at the core of everything we do.

If their mind is strong, there is nothing your children cannot achieve. So many people neglect the mind, ignoring it and treating it as simply part of our DNA, believing it will take care of itself. Not true.

The mind is like a muscle—it needs to be exercised regularly. If it doesn't get exercise, atrophy kicks in and we lose control of who we are and what we are doing.[8]

Developing the Masterpiece Mindset is a process, not a one-time event. It is a series of experiences, a childhood of experiences. A mindset that is built one brick at a time, day by day by day.

On many occasions, Michelangelo went into the Apuan Alps to the Carrara quarries to personally select the marble stone for his most famous masterpieces. He had two near-death experiences while slowly bringing the precious marble down the treacherous mountain paths.[9]

But throughout his life, Michelangelo's mindset was to do whatever it took to realize his vision for his masterpieces.

He was not immune to life's interruptions. In fact, it was quite the opposite. He used the time and tools he had available to create masterpiece after masterpiece.

The Masterpiece Mindset will give your children an amazing advantage in life and will allow them to maximize their own unique potential. They will not limit themselves, and will develop the motivation to find their own ceilings in life.

They will be empowered to sculpt their lives into masterpieces!

They will stand on their own two feet and have the ability to handle whatever comes their way. This independence comes from learning to act on the basis of what drives them from within, rather than what acts upon them from without.

What are the BENEFITS of building an Intentional Family Culture?

1. You establish a parenting vision with clear objectives.
2. You teach key principles that are most important to you.
3. You create an empowering environment in your home.
4. It significantly affects the way you see and teach your children.
5. You become an intentional parent rather than a reactive parent.
6. You maximize the likelihood of positive results for your children.
7. It is passed on to future generations of your family.

The whole objective of building an intentional family culture in your home is to empower your children to become who they are capable of becoming, whatever that looks like for them.

Your intentional family culture is the potential masterpiece you sculpt as a parent. It is your *David*.

Change your family culture slowly to make it permanent. You do that one small step at a time, by continuing to move, however slow, forward.

Complexity is the enemy of execution, so don't overthink it!

At the end of the day, the Masterpiece Mindset gives your children the ability to live a life that is a masterpiece. The intentional family culture you sculpt creates an environment that helps them get there.

You are Michelangelo and CAN empower your children to sculpt their lives into masterpieces!

We are excited to now introduce you to each of the seven key principles. Please take your time reading each chapter. Absorb the key principles carefully and thoughtfully and consider how each one of them can benefit your children and family right now.

Are you ready? Let's go!

 Dave and Annabella have a video message for you that relates to this chapter. Please go to **themasterpiecemindset.com** to view it.

BE WHAT
YOU CAN
SEE

BE WHAT YOU CAN SEE

"The poorest man is not he without a cent, it is he without a vision."
Old Chinese Proverb

JUST LIKE MICHELANGELO, YOUR CHILDREN's successful life journey begins with a vision of how they see themselves and their future possibilities. This key principle is the first step on their path to developing the Masterpiece Mindset.

Within your intentional family culture, your children can be taught to fiercely believe that they really can accomplish whatever they can see themselves doing.

"Whatever I can see in my mind, I can do and be." They can come to understand that they can create things in their mind and work to bring them into existence.

If your children have dreams but don't believe they can accomplish them, they are probably right—they won't. No one else has the right to tell your children what they are capable of. Do not put limits on their vision. Let them find out on their own where their ceiling is and what they are capable of.

Help your children to "see" their possibilities by celebrating and supporting any vision they develop for themselves. Affirming words from a mother and/or father are like a light switch and can reveal a room full of possibilities.

You begin to plant these seeds from an early age.

Regularly ask them these questions: "Who were you born to be?" "What were you born to do?" "Who are you capable of becoming?"

As one grandma said to her grandson on many occasions: "Go set the world on fire!" In other words, "I believe in you!"

Encourage them to shoot for the moon and wherever they end up is good enough.

Michelangelo used hammers and chisels as sculpting tools to create his marble masterpieces. Likewise, in each of the seven key principles chapters we will provide you with "sculpting tools" that you can use to introduce, teach, and reinforce each key principle to your children.

These sculpting tools become part of your parenting "tool bag," and work together to help your children learn, internalize, and live each of the seven key principles.

In this chapter, "Be What You Can See," the five sculpting tools are:

1. Foster Optimism
2. Celebrate Their Dreams
3. Inspire Them to Be a Dreamer and a Doer
4. Teach Them to Not Be Afraid of Standing Out
5. Change the Way They See Themselves

Sculpting Tool 1

Foster Optimism

What's most important is not what your children know, but what they believe about themselves.

Dr. Bob Rotella is one of America's preeminent psychologists. His book, *How Champions Think*, includes great insights about what goes on inside the minds of high achievers in all walks of life.

He says, "Any successful life starts with the way you see yourself."

Based on decades of professional experience, his opinion is that the first essential quality of high achievers is *optimism*:

> It's not something that's either in your genes or not in your genes, like blue eyes. I don't believe that people are born either optimistic or pessimistic the way you're born either right-handed or left-handed.
>
> Exceptional people, I have found, either start out being optimistic or learn to be optimistic because they realize that they can't get what they want in life without being optimistic.

Optimism is an attitude that people can choose to have. It's not always easy, but it can be done. Successful people I have worked with do it all the time. They choose optimism. Whatever happens to them, they find a reason to be hopeful.

Sometimes, after I give a talk, parents will approach me and say that they wish their kids had been present to hear it. Then they'll catch themselves and say, "Maybe it's just as well. I wouldn't want them to get big dreams, then be discouraged when they can't achieve them."

I can't help but think that these parents are going to raise the sort of children who, whatever their dreams might have been, will become people who just want to be safe and secure.

Optimism doesn't guarantee anything in life, but it will improve your chances. While the correlation between optimism and success is imperfect, there is an almost perfect correlation between negative thinking and failure.

So why wouldn't you be optimistic if it were a choice you could make?[1]

Here is a real-life example:

A man in his fifties was visiting with a teenager who lived in inner-city Los Angeles. When asked about his vision for his life, the young man matter-of-factly responded, "I'm either going to jail or I'm gonna die."

His answer was shocking, but odds were he was right—and those odds were increased by the fact that he was already laying out that path in his own mind. The man who asked the question could respond only by saying, "You're probably right. As long as that's the vision you hold for your life, that's likely what you will get."[2]

What your children *expect for themselves* in life is usually what they will get.

One set of parents we interviewed who have raised five well-adjusted, achieving children shared this with us: "My wife and I wanted to make sure we gave our children 'roots and wings' as a catalyst to creating empowering beliefs about themselves. The 'roots' are a sense of who they really are, a knowledge of their family heritage, and where they come from.

The 'wings' part allows them to take their own flight in life based on the confidence and vision we have tried to instill in them—the thing that is possible for each one of them."[3]

Sculpting Tool 2

Celebrate Their Dreams

Dreams are the starting point of any achievement.

Carli Lloyd, a former captain of the U.S. Women's Soccer team, said this: "You must be able to see it happening in your mind before it can happen on the field. The mind is like a brush-cutter in the woods, a bulldozer for your dreams.

It clears away the bramble and thicket so you have a path to follow. The mind sets out the path, and then the training enables you to follow it."[4]

Your children can develop the mentality of "Why *not* me?" One father consistently told his son as he was growing up, "Why not you?" That constant question and reminder inspired his son to dream bigger and work harder, and eventually led to his achieving incredible success in his chosen field.

When kids are young, they are often asked, "What do you want to be when you grow up?" What happens to these dreams as they get older? When do kids cross the magical boundary where they stop dreaming?

It happens when they're told they need to be more realistic or choose a "safer" path. Or maybe they are told what they've envisioned is too hard or that only "other" people can do those types of things.

Celebrate your children's dreams and validate their aspirations.

When your children tell you what they want to be or what they want to do in their lives, be different. Find opportunities to encourage their ambitions, even when they appear to be overreaching or unrealistic.

Every dreamer deserves a champion who will support them in their dreams. Let your children figure out for themselves what they can and can't do. Find ways to help them reach for and bump against their own ceilings.

Let them fly as far as their wings will take them.

A story is told as follows: A famous art professor died and went to heaven. At the pearly gates, the professor asked St. Peter, "Sir, I have spent most of my life on Earth studying great art, but I have a question that has puzzled me for over thirty years: Who was the greatest painter in history?"

St. Peter pointed to a nearby cloud. "See that woman right over there? She's the one."

The professor frowned. "But I knew that woman on Earth! She ran the cafeteria at the university where I taught? How could she have been the greatest painter in history?"

St. Peter shook his head sadly. "She could have been, if she would have ever picked up a brush and tried to paint."

I suspect that woman had been really good at her job, but did she reach her potential? Did she follow her passion? Was she content to let her dreams evaporate?[5]

Remind your children that "the only person who can limit your potential is you."

Become the parent who inspires their children to turn something that initially seems impossible into something possible. Ask, "What is something in your life that seems impossible right now? I wonder if you (or we) can figure out a way to make it possible?"

They can be taught to have the mindset that their "impossibles" can become "possible," whether it is to become a better reader, master a new skill, or anything else that is difficult for them.

The word "impossible" says it itself, "I'm possible!"

One of the most significant times during the day to have a powerful impact on your children's lives is early in the morning.

As your children leave your home each morning for school, help them feel invincible, as if they are ten feet tall and bulletproof. Start their day on fire by building them up so they feel empowered as they leave to take on their day.

One family we interviewed does a family cheer before their children go out the door in the morning.

One father we met told us this, "If my daughter can't dream big, ridiculous dreams, what's the point of her dreaming at all?" Try not to judge your children's dreams according to the odds of their coming true.

The real value of dreams lies in stirring within them the will to aspire.

Alexa von Tobel was the founder of LearnVest.com, an award-winning personal finance website. In 2006, as a recent college graduate, she was headed for a job with Morgan Stanley. And though she would soon be managing the bank's investments, she realized she didn't know the first thing about her own finances.

So she created LearnVest, an online personal finance resource for young women like herself. In 2015, after years of sustained growth, she sold LearnVest to Northwestern Mutual Life Insurance Company for a significant sum.

When asked to give career and life advice to recent college grads, she said, "The first thing is that you have to dream big because no one else can dream for you.

Now that I am becoming a new parent myself, *I'm trying to think about what my parents did to help me believe in myself.* I don't think I'm special in any way. I just believe in hard work, and I believe in dreaming big."[6]

SCULPTING TOOL 3

Inspire Them to Be a Dreamer and a Doer

Motivation is short-term; inspiration is long-term. You are the parent who inspires their children to become lifelong "dreamers and doers."

What could life be like for your children if they had a no-limits mindset? Could they maximize their potential and become who they are capable of becoming?

What they see, feel, and hear in your intentional family culture will have the most dramatic effect on what they come to believe about themselves. "You have the freedom to become whatever you have in you to become."

When you feel your children are ready, help them put together their first *bucket list*. A bucket list is nothing more than a written collection of hopes and dreams. Have fun with it!

To make it even more real, get an actual bucket for them (it can be small) and have them put their first bucket list in it! Put it somewhere they can see it. Get them excited about the possibilities for their future.

You might also consider putting together a *family bucket list* with your family's dreams and goals, and letting your children participate in the planning of its execution.

Let us introduce you to a real big dreamer, John Goddard, aka the "World's Greatest Goal Achiever." He is an interesting example of someone who wrote a bucket list at a fairly young age. When he was thirteen, he made a list of 127 things he wanted to do in his life.

Part of his list included exploring the Nile River; visiting Ethiopia, Kenya, Alaska, and other countries; climbing Mt. Everest; learning to fly an airplane; exploring the Great Barrier Reef in Australia; visiting the North and South poles; and climbing the Great Wall of China.

His list also included going to Vatican City and meeting the Pope; becoming an Eagle Scout; riding an elephant; skydiving; appearing in a Tarzan movie; learning French, Spanish, and Arabic; and milking a poisonous snake.

You get the message; he was a big dreamer. When he passed away in May 2013 at the age of eighty-eight, he had accomplished 120 of the 127 items on his original bucket list.

When asked what inspired his list, he gave all the credit to his parents. *"My parents gave me permission to be more,"* he said. "They introduced me to books in the library. I learned to love to read and imagine. These books opened up my mind to the possibilities for my life and helped me create a vision for myself.

My parents never stopped supporting me in my dreams."[7]

"I want this to be a good day, Mommy. Is this the right side of the bed for me to get up on?"

Author and biographer Irving Stone, who spent a lifetime studying great men and women in history, was once asked if he had found a common thread running through the lives of the exceptional people he examined.

He answered, "I write about people who sometime in life have a vision or dream of something that should be accomplished and they go to work.

They are beaten over the head, knocked down, vilified, and for years they get nowhere. But every time they're knocked down, they stand back up. You cannot destroy these people. And at the end of their lives they've accomplished some modest part of what they set out to do."[8]

Dreams don't mean a thing if they are not acted upon.

Here is an excerpt from an article written about major league baseball all-star Bryce Harper: "I was blown away by how comfortable he was in his own skin at age 16. He has a clear vision of who he is, where he wants to go, and how his enormous capacity for hard work is even more valuable than his great talent."[9]

Our guess is that the seeds of that vision, mindset, and work ethic were planted by his parents at an early age in their family culture.

Teach your children that their hopes and dreams are attainable only if they create a concrete plan or process to make them happen, and then go to work to execute their plan.

Nothing works without the work.

That's how you become a dreamer and a doer.

Everybody wants to be a great [fill in the blank] until it's time to do what it takes to become one. "Dreams won't work unless you do."

SCULPTING TOOL 4
Teach Them to Not Be Afraid of Standing Out

The following quote is frequently attributed to Nelson Mandela but was actually penned by author Marianne Williamson:

> Our deepest fear is not that we are inadequate. Our deepest fear is that we are powerful beyond measure. It is our light, not our darkness, that frightens us most. We ask ourselves, "Who am I to be brilliant, gorgeous, talented, fabulous?"
>
> Actually, who are you not to be? You are a child of God. Your playing small does not serve the world. There is nothing enlightened about shrinking so that other people won't feel insecure around you.
>
> We are all meant to shine. We were born to make manifest the glory of God that is within us. It's not just in some of us, it's in all of us.

And as we let our own light shine, we unconsciously give other people permission to do the same. As we are liberated from our own fear, our presence automatically liberates others.[10]

This kind of inner belief and mindset is life-altering for your children. Encourage them to take it to heart, maybe even memorize it, so that it eventually becomes part of their core identity and how they really see themselves.

Share with your children that God must have loved ordinary people because he made so many of us, but that every single day, all over the world, ordinary people are doing extraordinary things.

Encourage your children not to fear being unique or special. Share with them that "you don't need to ask for permission to be great, go take it."

To British politician Winston Churchill is attributed the quote: "To every man [and woman] there comes a moment when they are figuratively tapped on the shoulder and offered the chance to do a special thing unique to them. What a tragedy if that moment finds them unprepared or unqualified for that which could have been their finest hour."

One mother consistently put little reminder quotes in her kids' lunches when they were in elementary school. One of her sons, now in his thirties, has kept one of these notes in his wallet over the years.

Now tattered and worn, it reads, "Don't be afraid to be special!" It has served as a good reminder for him when he has needed it most.

Dr. Bob Rotella shares an additional bit of advice he gives clients: "It's a big advantage to aim high. When you aim high, you have a chance to be great. Even your failures will be better than most people's best. I counsel people to laugh at what other people perceive as failures.

I tell them not to care if other people think their goals are crazy. In fact, I tell them, if no one thinks your goals are crazy, you're probably not aiming high enough."[11]

Anthony Robles was born with one leg; none of the doctors could explain why. As he grew up, Anthony's mother taught him that God made him that way for a reason—and she helped Anthony believe it.

As a freshman in high school, Anthony joined the wrestling team. He was the smallest and worst wrestler on the team, and he placed last in the city wrestling tournament at the end of the season. Not many people believed that a tiny kid born with one leg could excel in such a demanding sport.

In fact, he and his mother were the only ones who believed he could—and they were right. In his junior and senior years at Mesa High School, he compiled a record of 96–0, became a two-time state champion, and won a national high school wrestling title.

In spite of that record, none of the established wrestling programs in America were interested in giving him a wrestling scholarship so Anthony decided to enroll at Arizona State University.

By the time his college career was complete, he was a three-time All-American and the 2011 NCAA national champion. He definitely stood out, both on and off the mat.

What made Anthony Robles a champion? He (and his mother) had a vision of his possibilities.

Every child deserves the chance to become somebody!

SCULPTING TOOL 5

Change the Way They See Themselves

The following story illustrates the application of this sculpting tool:

A father took his six-year-old daughter to a playground. The monkey bars had been a real challenge for her. She had tried many times to get all the way across, but on the second or third bar, she typically fell off.

This particular time she got to the fourth bar but slipped off again. She became discouraged and decided to stop trying. She wanted to quit.

At that moment, the father remembered an experience from a few weeks earlier. His daughter Tina had been trying to do something that was difficult for her. She wasn't able to do it, but she continued to try and try and try. Her dad had praised her consistent effort.

They decided to come up with an animal nickname that would represent her physical and mental strength—a fearless animal—so as to help her see herself in a different way.

She became Tiger Tina!

So on this day, as the father watched his daughter struggle with the monkey bars, he asked her a question: "I wonder if Tiger Tina can do it?" His daughter hesitated, thought for a moment, and then got back up on the monkey bars. She confidently and boldly went all the way across for the first time in her life.

When she finished, she yelled, "I did it!" Her dad again praised her effort and said, "Nice job, Tiger Tina!" and they loudly and proudly celebrated her accomplishment together.

What created this dramatic transformation in Tina's mindset? Simply put, her father helped her to see herself differently. In that moment, her identity had changed. She first began to see herself as a tiger and then acted like one. She first believed she could go all the way across the monkey bars, then did it.

When she returned home, she shared the experience with her mom, which further reinforced her Tiger Tina persona. She was on the road to gradually changing the way she saw herself. Given future "Tiger Tina" experiences, she can permanently make that mental pivot and create new inner beliefs and core identity.

The way your children see themselves will be reflected in the way they act.

Most children enjoy animals. Talk to your children about what kind of animal they would like to be and why. Invite them to choose an animal that is strong and helps them feel courageous and brave.

Or maybe they would prefer to be a favorite superhero, like Superman, Batman, Wonder Woman, Black Panther, Batwoman, Wolverine, Storm, or Spiderman. It makes no difference what or who the "alter-ego" identity is as long as it helps your children channel their inner strength, persistence, and resilience.

Once they have a vision of what is possible for themselves, their motivation to achieve comes from the inside. Real confidence and mental strength is generated from within, not without.

At the end of the day, your children will only be as strong and confident as their mind allows them to be.

What are the BENEFITS of "Be What You Can See" for your children?

1. They develop a vision of what's possible for them.
2. They develop an optimistic attitude toward life.
3. They become dreamers and doers.
4. They are not afraid to stand out.
5. They are easier to parent!

Ten-Second Summary

Be What You Can See

1. Foster Optimism
2. Celebrate Their Dreams
3. Inspire Them to Be a Dreamer and a Doer

4. Teach Them to Not Be Afraid of Standing Out
5. Change the Way They See Themselves

The purpose of this chapter is for this principle to eventually become a deeply rooted inner belief, Belief 1 (below), within the minds and hearts of your children.

This belief will reflect how they see, feel, and think about themselves and become part of their core identity. In other words, this is who **I AM.**

BELIEF 1

**"I AM a person who can be
what I can see in my mind."**

OUR INVITATION

As you complete this chapter, what do you feel inspired to do right now to incorporate this key principle of "Be What You Can See" into the lives of your children? As a starting point, we invite you to list your initial thoughts or ideas here:

1.

2.

3.

OUR PROMISE

This "Be What You Can See" mindset can become an important element of your family DNA and intentional family culture. It is a critical first step in creating a core identity for your children that leads them to developing the Masterpiece Mindset.

Your children do not have to sit in the passenger seat of life. They have the opportunity to be the driver of their lives—and it starts with their vision, thoughts, and inner beliefs about themselves, and their future.

They can become who they are capable of becoming.

If you begin planting the seeds of this key principle from an early age, trust us—you will enjoy the results! Someone once said, "Give a child a match and he'll be warm for a minute, but set him on fire and he'll be warm for the rest of his life."

You are the parent who ignites that fire within your children's minds and hearts!

You are Michelangelo and CAN empower your children to sculpt their lives into Masterpieces!

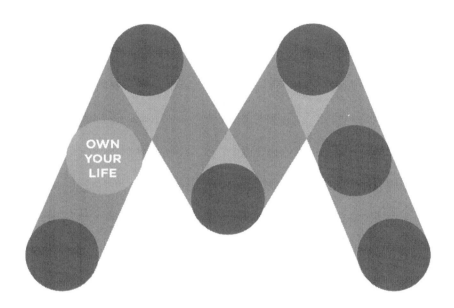

OWN
YOUR
LIFE

PRINCIPLE 2

OWN YOUR LIFE

"If people knew how hard I worked to get my mastery,
it wouldn't seem so wonderful at all."
Michelangelo

THIS SECOND KEY PRINCIPLE HELPS children internalize that they are ultimately responsible for how their life turns out. They are taught to take ownership of their lives and the decisions they make. "Whatever you do, it's up to you."

Help your children understand how important it is to not make excuses or blame others when things don't go their way. Create an intentional "no-excuse" family culture in your home. They, and only they, are the authors of their life's narrative, and write their own story.

Color of skin, family income level, neighborhood, quality of school, family dynamic—it makes no difference. Regardless of their circumstances, it is *their* responsibility, not someone else's, to become the best version of themselves.

That said, let's not forget that children who experience significant mental or physical health challenges will probably experience a very different journey, and that is perfectly fine. They still can become who THEY are capable of becoming.

As sixteenth century French essayist Michel de Montaigne remarked, "Not being able to govern events, I govern myself." Sometimes life will simply deal your children a difficult hand. Encourage them to "play the hand you're dealt the best you can, because that's all you can do."

Others may (and certainly do) have an easier path in life, but it doesn't matter. It just is what it is.

Life is simply not fair, but it can still be good.

Your children's path to personal empowerment and the Masterpiece Mindset lies in taking personal responsibility for their own life. Teach your children that "you are accountable for who and what you become."

As musician Jon Butcher put it, "Your life is yours. You own it. You choose whom you spend time with. You choose the books you read and the TV shows you watch. You choose the way you treat people. You can choose to live any way you want to live.

You can choose where you want to live. You can choose to do anything you want to do. You can choose to be any kind of person you want to be. You can shape your life any way you want to shape it."

Help your children understand that "Performance wins out in the end. Other people's preconceptions can make it more difficult to gain an opportunity, but once you get your chance, it's up to you what you do with it."

A mother shared this with us as she gazed fondly at her young son:

"Isn't it crazy that this little person right here will be among the future leaders of the world? He could be a future scientist, artist, teacher, entrepreneur, or whatever he wants to be—changing and influencing the world with a huge impact someday.

If we always looked at our children this way—I think we would be more aware of how we treat them, what we speak to them, and how it's affecting their mindset and development.

Let's create the leaders of the world! Let's teach our children that they are the ones in control of their lives—no one else."

Teach your children: "You determine who you are. You determine who you become, not someone else."

As your children begin to internalize this key principle, it will eventually become the way they see themselves and their futures.

They learn to own who they are. That doesn't mean you are not there to support them; of course you are. What it does mean is that they get in the habit of doing whatever they can on their own from an early age.

Encourage them to own their mistakes, and edit their behavior when necessary. Identifying their contribution to setbacks will not only help your children avoid future problems but keep failure from spawning victimhood.

This ownership mindset gives children a tremendous advantage in the real world as so few people are willing to accept personal responsibility for their mistakes.

Lack of personal ownership halts progress dead in its tracks.

Throughout the rest of this chapter, we share five sculpting tools to help you introduce and teach this key principle to your children. These tools work together to make personal ownership an integral component of your children's mindset and core identity.

They are:

1. Find a Way
2. Hopes and Dreams Are Made True
3. If You Don't Grind, You Don't Shine
4. You Are What You Do
5. Be a Finisher

SCULPTING TOOL 1

Find a Way

Teach your children that no matter what obstacles they face, they can find a way to get things done. If something is important enough to them, they'll find a way. If not, they'll find an excuse. As inventor Benjamin

Franklin once said, "He that is good at making excuses is seldom good for anything else."

Here is an excellent example from U.S. history. In 1899, President William McKinley needed to deliver an urgent message to General Calixto Garcia, leader of the insurgents in America's war against Spain. But Garcia was lost somewhere deep in the mountains of Cuba—no one knew where.

When President McKinley announced that he had a critically important message he needed delivered to Garcia, he was told a Colonel Andrew Rowan could find Garcia, if anyone could. So McKinley summoned Rowan to his office.

Rowan took McKinley's letter, "sealed in an oilskin pouch," and strapped it over his heart. Four days later, he landed by night in an open boat off the coast of Cuba and disappeared into the jungle.

After three weeks, he came out on the other side of the island, having traversed a hostile country on foot and finally delivered the letter to Garcia.

Rowan didn't ask where Garcia might be found; he didn't shrink from the difficulty of the assignment or ask for detailed instructions. He didn't ask for any special resources, he didn't hire a consultant or assemble a task force, and he certainly didn't complain.

He simply took the letter and found a way to deliver it.[1] Your children can develop the same resolute mindset as Colonel Rowan.

We have a friend whose son enjoyed school and worked hard to do well. He had been an A student in middle school and was also a skilled basketball player. When the time came for high school, he was excited to play on his high school basketball team.

Before he entered ninth grade, his parents discussed with him the importance of his grades as they related to getting into the college of his choice. They asked him what grades he thought he should achieve so that he could qualify for the *privilege* of playing basketball.

Learning and academics were important in their family culture, and he knew it. The boy said, "I earned all As in middle school, so I think I have the ability and study habits to get As in high school as well." So they struck a deal. If he didn't get As in all of his classes, he couldn't play basketball for his school.

He had set the academic bar for himself and was willing to hold himself accountable. He became the starting point guard for his school's ninth-grade team and was excited for the season to begin.

A week before the first game, he found out he had an issue in one of his classes. He came home from school and said to his father, "Dad, I have a little problem. I have an A- in art, but I'm only one point away from an A. That's not a big deal, right? It's just art."

His dad smiled and asked him, "Is art a class you actually go to?"

His son responded, "Yes, it is."

"Well," his father said, "then it is a real class, and it counts. You know the agreement we have, and it was your idea. If you don't have an A, you can't play in the game next week. Why don't you just go talk to the teacher and see if you can do some extra credit for that one point?"

The next day, the young man talked to his art teacher before class began: "I am one point from getting an A in this class, and if I don't get an A, I can't play in the basketball game next week. Is there any extra credit work I could do to make up the one point?"

The teacher turned to the class and said, "Bill is one point from getting an A in this class, and if he doesn't get an A, he can't play in the basketball game next week. What should I have him do to earn that one point?"

Someone in the back of the classroom yelled, "Fifty push-ups!"

The teacher looked at Bill and said, "Okay, that will work." Bill dropped down in front of the class and did the push-ups as his classmates cheered him on. He earned the one point he needed, got the A, and played in the game!

The young man and his dad laugh about the memory to this day.

Bill had found a way to get the job done.

Dr. Carol S. Dweck, a psychology professor at Stanford University and author of the influential book *Mindset*, has been researching motivation and perseverance in children since the 1960s.

She once asked herself, "Why do some kids give up easily when faced with difficulty while others who are no more skilled continue to strive and learn?" She discovered it depends on the student's beliefs on *why* he or she failed.

Dweck proposed that there are two basic mindsets: a fixed mindset and a growth mindset.

Those with a *fixed mindset* believe their successes are a result of the natural talent or smarts they are born with—that one is either good at something or not.

These people believe they are "stuck" with whatever intelligence they are born with and there is nothing they can do to enhance it. In fact, when they don't do well at something, they quickly give up. As a result, they avoid challenges, fearful they won't "look smart."

These people assume traits are inherent and cannot be changed. The problem with the fixed mindset is the belief that a negative outcome is a reflection on a person's very nature. If this person fails an exam, this mindset says it is because "I am not intelligent."

Those with a *growth mindset* believe their successes are a result of their effort and work ethic. They believe they can get good at something through practice over time.

They feel that everyone, even the "geniuses" of the world, must work hard and apply themselves, especially when they run into difficulty. They value learning more than looking smart. They keep pushing when situations are the toughest.

They take personal ownership of situations and find a way to get things done.[2]

Sculpting Tool 2

Hopes and Dreams Are Made True

Dreams don't come true by chance—they come true by choice.

Dreamers become doers when they have a plan or process for how to reach their goals and then go to work.

Imagine a pilot coming over the intercom and announcing, "I have some good news and some bad news. The bad news is that we have lost one engine and the plane's direction finder.

The good news is that we have a tail wind and wherever we are going we are getting there at a rate of 600 miles per hour."

Many people are like this pilot. They often fly along in life directionless, being pushed swiftly along by the winds of circumstance to an unknown destination.[3]

That will not be your children.

In your intentional family culture, your children learn to start setting goals early. For example, let's say your third-grade daughter comes home from school and announces she wants to participate in her class spelling bee.

You first validate and celebrate her desire to participate! Then you help her figure out a plan or process that will help her do her very best.

Let her drive the process as much as possible; you are the support team. It really doesn't matter how well she does or doesn't do in the actual spelling bee. She's experienced the goal-setting process and learned more spelling words than if she did not participate.

And she can now duplicate that same process for other goals in her future.

Your children can become intentional in the way they approach their life. Being intentional is empowering and builds real confidence within them.

Teach your children that those who accomplish most in life have goals, and a process for how to achieve those goals. Your son or daughter can become a lifelong goal setter and process creator.

A goal without a plan is just a wish.

Knowing where they are going and how they expect to get there increases their odds of success. A goal is the destination. The plan or process is the route by which they get there. The goal can be clear, but there has to be a solid process to get there.

Dr. Rotella continues: "Without a dream, it's hard to be motivated. But it's also true that dreams are cheap. Lots of people who never achieve much have dreams. Exceptional people also have dreams. But exceptional people go well beyond dreaming.

The ability to take a dream and use it to create a process is what separates exceptional people from mere dreamers. Without making and sustaining a commitment to an effective process, an individual cannot know her potential."[4]

Learning how to develop a process and then execute it will be a life changer that will benefit your children their whole lives. As your children think about their goals, teach them to focus on the process that actually gives them the best chance of reaching their goals.

Commit to the process.

Every process begins with taking the sometimes difficult first step, and then continuing by completing one more step at a time.

Nothing ever changes without movement. A single action can open doors we would never imagine. Help your children to "never be afraid to take a chance and take that first small step."

In other words, dream big, start small.

For example, imagine trying to cross a river that is shallow but very fast and dangerous. If you look across toward the opposite shore and see the potential risk of the powerful flowing water, you might decide to turn around and give up any thought of attempting to cross.

However, if you look around the bank where you are standing and find a single stepping-stone, you could put that first stone in the water close to the shore where you are standing. Then, using that first stone, you could place another stone, and so on.

Before you know it, you would have reached the other side of the river by keeping your focus on each little step you need to take. You will have left little room for your fears to derail you.

We often think our goals are insurmountable, when in fact they are only one small step away. Great things are possible for your children by having them take one small step at a time and staying locked in on that process.

You can begin by having your children set goals that are small enough to win but big enough to matter. Once they begin to string together several wins, they can set bigger goals that stretch them beyond their perceived capacity.

Consistency creates momentum. Breaking down a process into small steps or habits and working on them every day creates belief in self, where there might have been self-doubt at the beginning.

Focusing on the process will give your children the best chance of getting where they want to go in life, and actually achieving some measure of their hopes and dreams.

As they take ownership of their goals, amazing things can happen, so make goal setting and process creating a focus of your intentional family culture: "We [insert your family name here] are a goal-setting and process-creating family. That's just who we are and what we do."

Here is an excellent model you can adapt and simplify to fit any goal-setting experience in your home.

1. **Write down your goal** in clear, articulate language that describes **EXACTLY** what you hope to achieve with a **deadline** for its achievement.

2. **Develop a plan or process** that provides a detailed framework for **HOW** you will achieve your goal.

3. In advance, understand and **detail any obstacles** that could prevent you from achieving your goal. Develop solutions in advance that will resolve your concerns and clear a pathway to achieving your goal.

4. **Set up checkpoints along the way.** Break your overall process down into smaller, bite-sized, chewable chunks that permit you to see you are on schedule, and making progress toward achieving your objectives.

5. **Is it worth it to you?** Will the sacrifice outweigh the achievement of the goal? Are you absolutely certain the ladder you are climbing has been set against the right wall?[5]

What if all of your children's dreams don't come true? Would it be better for them to not have lofty goals so they are not disappointed? No way. The best-laid plans hardly ever go smoothly.

Successfully learning to deal with disappointment is an empowering life skill that creates deeply rooted resilience within your children.

What is resilience? It is defined as "an ability to recover from or adjust easily to misfortune or change."[6] Resilience cannot be created in a vacuum. It is developed only through experiences that create it.

Let your children struggle and fail.

The fact that a specific goal is not realized should not detract from the educational value of the experience. Sometimes it's just necessary for them to set a new goal—a plan B. They can then turn a disappointing exit into a successful entrance.

Everybody can touch the stars, but it may not be the star they envisioned.

If they have executed their process to the best of their ability, wherever it takes them is good enough. Your children should understand that as long as they did everything in their power to go for it, they really are true champions and winners.

You should loudly and proudly celebrate their effort.

Dr. Rotella adds, "I have no trouble with someone who strives to be the best and finishes in the middle of the pack. There's honor in that. I don't see that person as a failure. To the contrary, he will come to the end of his days with a smile on his face because he spent the time and talent that God gave him having a ball, *finding out how good he could be.*"[7]

Sculpting Tool 3
If You Don't Grind, You Don't Shine

Always celebrate what you want your children to value, especially when they've worked hard and put forth sincere effort. Plant the seeds when they are young that the only difference between ordinary and extraordinary is a little "extra." And what about luck?

Luck is the residue of intentional, sustained effort.

Though Michelangelo was only five feet four inches tall and weighed slightly north of one hundred pounds, his workload was legendary. It took him over four years to complete the ceiling of the Sistine Chapel. Speaking of that incredible undertaking, it was said:

> He grew dizzy from standing with his head and shoulders thrown back, his neck arched so that he could peer straight upward, his arms aching in every joint from the vertical effort, his eyes blurred from the dripping paint even though he had learned to paint through slits and to blink them shut with each brush stroke.
>
> He would sometimes paint sitting down, his thighs drawn up tight against his belly for balance, his eyes a few inches from the ceiling, until the unpadded bones of his buttocks became so bruised and sore that he could no longer endure the agony.
>
> Then he would lie flat on his back, his knees in the air, doubled over as tightly as possible against his chest to steady his painting arm, so that he could keep going.[8]

Your children can take pride in being known as hard workers, or "grinders."

Make hard work a centerpiece of your intentional family culture: "We [insert your family name here] work hard at everything we do. It's just who we are."

It will become part of your children's core identity and how they see themselves. Help them understand that nobody goes from "zero to hero" without the benefit of hard work.

Jonathan, a brilliant student, sailed through grade school. He completed his assignments easily and routinely earned As. When Jonathan puzzled over why some of his classmates struggled, his parents told him he had a special gift.

In the seventh grade, however, Jonathan suddenly lost interest in school, refusing to do homework or study for tests. As a consequence, his grades plummeted. His parents tried to boost his confidence by assuring him he was smart.

But their attempts failed to motivate Jonathan (who is a composite of several children). Schoolwork, their son maintained, was boring and pointless.

Our society worships talent, and many assume that possessing superior intelligence or ability—along with confidence in that ability—is a recipe for success.

However, more than thirty-five years of scientific investigation suggests that an overemphasis on intellect or talent leaves people vulnerable to failure, fearful of challenges, and unwilling to remedy shortcomings.

The results play out in children like Jonathan, who coast through the early grades under the dangerous notion that no-effort academic achievement defines them as smart or gifted. Such children hold an implicit belief that intelligence is innate and fixed, which makes striving to learn seem far less important than being (or looking) smart.

This belief also makes challenges, mistakes, and even the need to exert effort appear as threats to their ego rather than opportunities to improve. And it causes them to lose confidence and motivation when the work is no longer easy.[9]

Talent is great, who doesn't wish they were born with special talent? But it doesn't matter. Teach your children that the people willing to put in the work, to do the most with what they have been given, are those who will ultimately become who they are capable of becoming.

People do differ in natural intelligence, talent, and ability. And yet research is converging on the conclusion that great accomplishment, and even what we call genius, is typically the result of years of passion and dedication and not something that flows naturally.

Mozart, Edison, Curie, Darwin, and Cezanne were not simply born with talent; they cultivated it through tremendous, sustained effort.[10]

We recently saw an inspiring example of hardworking young people. A young family in our neighborhood has three children ages thirteen, eleven, and eight. After an activity in the cultural hall at our church, Dave was assigned to put away approximately 250 chairs and twenty large tables by loading them onto specially constructed racks.

It turned out to be a lengthy project since the adults who were supposed to come help him did not show up.

As Dave began to fold the chairs, he looked around and saw these three kids doing the same thing. No one had said a word to them; they just saw Dave needed help and jumped in. Dave could not believe how they persevered to lift the heavy tables and put them on the rack.

They worked with an intensity and focus that was impressive. At several points, Dave asked them, "Would you like some help?" Every time they would say, "No, we're good."

They worked until every last chair and table was folded and loaded onto the racks. Dave later saw their parents, shared the experience with them, and complimented them on raising such hardworking kids. They just smiled and thanked Dave as if it were no big deal.

Working hard and recognizing when help was needed were clearly an expected element of their intentional family culture. Nice job Mom and Dad!

Teach your children that: "If you want something, go make it happen. It's not anyone else's job." The only place success comes before work is in the dictionary.

There is no elevator to success; you have to take the stairs. Your children can come to clearly understand that if they want to become the best version of themselves, they need to become grinders.

In other words, "do what is required, do the work, do what you said you would do."

Sculpting Tool 4

You Are What You Do

It has been said that the door of history turns on small hinges, and so it will be for each of your children. As American politician William Jennings Bryan wrote, "Destiny is not a matter of chance; it is a matter of choice."[11]

Please teach your children that it's not what they *think* about doing or *talk* about doing that matters—it's what they *actually* do. As Greek storyteller Aesop famously said, "When all is said and done, more is said than done."

Simply said, you are what you do.

If you were to take any sort of object and drop it, what would happen? It would fall straight to the ground, regardless of whether it was a ball, a rock, or a feather. Why? Because of the universal law of gravity, right? Whatever goes up will always come down.

The same natural law applies to your children's choices and habits. Every choice they make or habit they create comes with consequences, whether they like them or not.

Help them understand that they are free to make any choice or develop any habit they want, but they are not free to choose the consequences that come attached to that choice or habit.

Life is nothing more than a series of choices.

Your children can learn to be intentional about their choices. In other words, "When you choose the road, you choose the destination." The earlier in life they learn this, the better.

Help your children understand that choices are inherently good or bad, regardless of whether they are popular. One parent we interviewed taught her children, "If it's right and no one else is doing it, it's still right. If it's wrong and everyone is doing it, it's still wrong."

Teach your children the value of choosing the harder right instead of the easier wrong.

**"Conscience is like Mommy tellin'
you not to do somethin',
but she isn't there."**

Life coach Brenda Slavin wrote, "Everything you do is based on the choices you make. It's not your parents, your past relationships, your job, the economy, or your age that is to blame. You, and only you, are responsible for every decision and choice you make. Period."

Please let your children experience the natural consequences of their choices.

Do not bail them out if they make a wrong choice. We know it's difficult; your first impulse as a parent is to rescue and save the day. We get it, but unless your children's well-being is in jeopardy, let them suffer the natural consequences that come with negative choices.

If you do bail them out, they will be learning the wrong lesson. It is not how the real world works, and can inhibit your children's ability to become competent adults.

They need to clearly understand that in life, they will generally reap what they sow.

The earlier they figure this out, the better. Your children will suffer much less serious long-term damage that way.

One set of parents took this approach: "We loved the children regardless of what they did but would not prevent the consequences of any of their actions. *We let them suffer natural consequences* and did not try to mitigate the consequences because we saw them suffering.

We would cry and be sad but would not do anything to reduce the consequences of their actions. They needed to learn. From our perspective, the sooner they learned, the better."

One of our sons worked hard in high school and was accepted into Princeton University in New Jersey. He received his acceptance package in early February of his senior year. Once he received his letter, he felt like he was done with school, that he didn't need to attend his classes anymore.

We reminded him that his Princeton acceptance was subject to a review of his last-term grades. The invitation could be rescinded. But he didn't really take us seriously and attended his classes sporadically from that point on.

Our school district had a strict attendance policy. If a student had earned an A in a class but did not attend a certain amount of days within the term period, they could still be given an F and not receive credit toward graduation. We regularly reminded our son of this policy.

He said he was not concerned and could work things out with his teachers because he knew the material and had earned As in all his classes.

A week before graduation, his history teacher told him he would be receiving an F because he had not attended often enough to get credit. The teacher was an assistant basketball coach at the school, and our son was an all-state basketball player.

Our son thought the coach would "take care of him" because of that relationship, but the coach did not. And our son needed credit for that last class in order to graduate.

That afternoon, he came home very upset and said, "Dad, you need to talk to Coach Schoonover. He won't give me credit for my history class, and if I don't get credit for it, I can't graduate."

Inside I smiled, and thought to myself, *What a great teaching opportunity!*

I said to my son, "Why are you surprised? You know the district's attendance policy, and Mom and I warned you often that this could happen. There is no way I am talking to Coach Schoonover. In fact, I am glad he is enforcing the rules. This is a great life lesson for you."

He was not happy with me.

The next week his class graduated. Without him. Talk about being embarrassed. We even tried talking him into attending the graduation ceremony, hoping he would feel the consequence of his negligence ever more poignantly, but he said, "no way."

People stopped by our house that evening and asked about him, thinking he was ill. We would go upstairs and get him, then let *him* tell them the story, which caused him even greater embarrassment.

It was a painful but necessary learning experience for him.

What's the end of the story? He retook the history class during the summer and got an A. At the end of the summer, he left to do service work for our church in Brazil. For the two years he was gone, he wondered if Princeton would honor his acceptance when they saw the F.

He agonized about whether he would be able to attend Princeton after four years of very hard work in high school. He was fortunate. They held his spot, and he was able to attend upon his return home.

Natural consequences are a great teacher.

He has *never* forgotten that lesson.

Be careful not to overparent your children, to become a so-called "snowplow" parent. Snowplow parents go to great lengths to remove obstacles from their children's path, which robs them of the necessary experience of learning and failing.

It reminds us of the parents who got caught up in the 2019 college-admissions scandal who ended up serving time behind bars for their well-intentioned but badly executed attempt to help their children.

"Snowplow parents have it backward. The point is to prepare the kid for the road, instead of preparing the road for the kid."[12]

As author Hara Marano stated in her book, *A Nation of Wimps,* "Overprotected and over-managed by their parents, and with few challenges all their own through which to sharpen their instincts and identities, kids are unable to forge their own unique adaptations to the normal vicissitudes of life. That not only makes them extraordinarily risk-adverse; it makes them psychologically fragile."[13]

We promise you that in the end, you will regret choosing that parenting model.

Perhaps this is one of the factors why the anxiety, depression and suicide statistics are through the roof for children, adolescents and young adults.

Anxiety disorders affect 25.1 percent of children between 13 and 18 years old. Research shows that children with anxiety disorders who are left untreated are at higher risk to perform poorly in school, miss out on important social experiences, and engage in substance abuse.[14]

In 2017, 2.3 million adolescents had at least one episode of severe depression impairment, and 9.4 percent of the population ages 12 to 17 experienced clinical depression.[15]

According to a 2016 American College Health Association (ACHA) survey, almost 37 percent of college students reported feeling so depressed at some point during the previous year they found it difficult to function.[16]

College mental-health counseling centers all over the United States are bursting at the seams as they cannot meet the demand for therapy services.

Suicide rates among teens and young adults have reached their highest point in nearly two decades according to a study highlighted in *Journal of the American National Medical Association*. Suicides among teens have especially spiked, with an annual percentage change of 10 percent between 2014 and 2017 for 15- to 19-year-olds.

"It really is an unprecedented surge," said the study's lead author, Oren Mirron, a research associate at Harvard Medical School in Boston. "You can go back decades and you won't find such a sharp increase."[17]

According to the Centers for Disease Control and Prevention (CDC) 2017 Youth Risk Behavior Data Summary and Trends Report 2007–2017,

32% of high school students experienced ongoing feelings of sadness and hopelessness
17% said they seriously considered suicide
14% made a suicide plan
7% tried to kill themselves[18]

In 2017, there were 6,252 suicides in the 15- to 24-year-old age group, which was the second leading cause of death in that demographic.[19]

These are startling and alarming trends and statistics.

Why is this happening in the lives of our children and young adults today?

We don't have the space in this book to fully address all of the potential reasons. However, what we can say is that helping your children learn to do hard things, handle failure successfully, and develop increased resilience will make them more anxiety, depression, and suicide resistant.

Though children may be born with a genetic predisposition toward anxiety or depression, *parents can create an environment in their home where that predisposition is not magnified.*

Prepare your children for the path, not the path for your children.

Consider becoming a "safety-net" parent. Safety-net parents allow their children to solve their own problems to the extent they can but then make themselves available when necessary for emergency situations.

The **important point** is this: If you make life *easy* for your kids when they are young, they will make life *challenging* for you when they get older. If you make life *challenging* for your kids when they are young, they will make life *easier* for you when they are older.

As a parent, YOU get to make that choice.

The quality and trajectory of your children's lives will also be directly affected by their choice of habits, which will either bring them closer to or further away from making their vision for themselves a reality.

Their habits will determine the difference between who they are and who they could be.

Your children can "win the day" by developing intentional habits, and internalizing the notion that self-discipline is at the root of all good things.

As University of Alabama football coach Nick Saban has said, "You can either suffer the pain of discipline or the pain of disappointment." Your children's habits say to the world and themselves, "This is who I am and what I do every day."

We all eventually become our habits.

Greek philosopher Aristotle said this about habits: "We are what we repeatedly do. Excellence then is not an act, but a habit." Help your children understand that as they develop productive daily habits, they are investing in themselves and in their future.

Behavior that is rewarded is repeated.

Celebrate and reinforce your children's positive habits. They first form their habits and then their habits form them. Their habits create results. Positive habits create positive results. Positive habits lead to increased empowerment, confidence, and added resilience.

As life coach Seth Ellsworth once shared, "Win the battle today, and the outcome of the war is certain."

This "habit training" can begin at a young age.

Dr. Rotella shares additional counsel: "Habits are powerful forces in our lives. When we act from habit, we don't need the grit-your-teeth type of willpower. We just do something without thinking much about it. It's almost a reflex.

Exceptional people tend to have habits that help them achieve what they want. People who are struggling tend to have habits that undermine them."[20]

Habits are habit forming, and good habits are just as hard to break as bad habits!

Periodically ask your children, "Are the habits you have today going to lead you to the hopes and dreams you have for yourself tomorrow?" And remind them often that "he who conquers himself is greater than he who conquers an army."

Choices and habits—you are what you do.

Sculpting Tool 5

Be a Finisher

Encourage your children to be a finisher in everything they do.

Quitting should not be an easy option in your intentional family culture. The nature of the task doesn't matter; the point is to finish what they start so they feel that hit of accomplishment at the end.

Dave once had an interesting conversation with one of our nephews who was just finishing his junior year of high school. Dave asked if he was looking forward to his senior year. He had played on his school's football team for the first three years of high school.

Dave asked if he was excited about playing his final year. He told Dave he was not going to play, and Dave said, "Why not?"

He replied, "I don't think I will get much playing time because there are other players on the team who are better than me, so I don't see the point of wasting all that time just practicing."

Dave asked him, "So what will you do with all your extra time if you quit the team?"

He said, "I don't really know because I have plenty of time to get my homework done even when I am playing football."

Dave invited him to sit down so they could talk through his decision to quit before he actually did it. Dave pointed out, "You've already invested three years in football; maybe you should consider finishing what you started.

I understand that you want to play in the games—everybody does—but sometimes we don't get everything we want in life." Dave then asked, "Are there any other benefits to being on the team other than just playing in the games on Friday nights?"

The young man thought for a moment and responded, "Well, I would continue to stay in great shape. I also have many good friends on the team, and I do enjoy being part of a winning program.

I guess it's possible that if I continue to work hard in practice, I might actually get better and possibly get some playing time." Dave said, "And don't forget you would also have a great seat at the games on the sidelines!"

Our nephew soon began to see that the football experience was about much more than just playing in the games. The whole of the experience was better than just that one part.

He and Dave then talked about the importance of finishing what we start in life and that if he quit football now, it would be easier for him to quit something else in the future.

After analyzing all the benefits, he decided to play football in his senior year and to finish what he started. Dave was proud of him and told him so.

Fast-forward one year. Our nephew's team won the state championship, and he was able to play in almost every game, including the state semifinal game. It turned out to be a mature decision to see his football career through to the end, and he really enjoyed the experience.

We hope his decision to be a finisher will help our nephew finish more difficult endeavors ahead of him in life.

Check out his state championship ring!

And talk about finishers. As evening fell in Mexico City in 1968, John Stephen Akhwari of Tanzania painfully hobbled into the Olympic Stadium—the last man to finish the punishing 26.2 mile marathon.

The victory ceremony for the winning runner was long over, and the stadium was almost empty as Akhwari, his leg bloody and bandaged, struggled to circle the track and cross the finish line.

When asked why he had continued the grueling run to the finish line after being seriously injured in the race, the young man did not have to search for an answer. He said, "My country did not send me 5,000 miles to start the race. They sent me 5,000 miles to *finish* the race."[21]

We honor and respect the "finishers" in life.

What are the BENEFITS of "Own Your Life" for your children?

1. They learn to take ownership of their lives.
2. Negative peer pressure becomes less of an issue for them.
3. They become self-motivated hard workers.
4. They set goals and create processes for achieving their goals.
5. They don't make excuses, and they find ways to get things done.

6. They understand the benefits of good choices and habits.
7. Life is much easier for you as their parent!

Ten-Second Summary

Own Your Life

1. Find a Way
2. Hopes and Dreams Are Made True
3. If You Don't Grind, You Don't Shine
4. You Are What You Do
5. Be a Finisher

The purpose of this chapter is for this principle to eventually become a deeply rooted inner belief, Belief 2 (below), within the minds and hearts of your children.

This belief will reflect how they see, feel, and think about themselves and become part of their core identity. In other words, this is who **I AM.**

BELIEF 2

"I AM the owner of my life."

OUR INVITATION

We invite you to record any thoughts or impressions you have received by reading and considering the key principle of "Own Your Life." Are there ways you can begin to plant the seeds of the five sculpting tools in your family culture right now?

1.

2.

3.

OUR PROMISE

As your children acquire an "Own Your life" mindset and realize they are in control of their lives, their future will feel and look different. They acquire the confidence to "own" their lives and "who they are."

That is powerful.

As they come to embrace and live this principle, your children are bringing themselves closer to developing the Masterpiece Mindset and experiencing a masterpiece of a life.

You are Michelangelo and CAN empower your children to sculpt their lives into Masterpieces!

DON'T BE
AFRAID
TO FAIL

Don't Be Afraid to Fail

"The greatest risk to man is not that he aims too high and misses, but that he aims too low and hits."
Michelangelo

THIS THIRD KEY PRINCIPLE, "DON'T Be Afraid to Fail," has the power to dramatically change the trajectory of your children's lives. It provides them with deep confidence and increased resilience, opens new worlds of possibility, and is a catalyst for becoming the best version of themselves.

We cannot overemphasize how critical it is for your children to learn, internalize, and live this key principle. Without it, it will be impossible for them to develop the Masterpiece Mindset.

Once, when one of our granddaughters was visiting, we watched her try to put together a puzzle. At only three years of age, the puzzle was difficult for her, and she became frustrated. She finally threw all the puzzle pieces up in the air and yelled, "I can't do it!"

Dave asked her if she would like some help, and she reluctantly said yes. With a little coaching from Dave, they completed the puzzle together. Dave then encouraged her to do the puzzle again, this time by herself.

When she finished, she looked at Dave and said excitedly, "Grandpapa, I did it!"

Dave smiled, gave her a high five, and then asked, "Would you like to try another one?" She replied, "Sure." She had found the confidence to take on new, challenging puzzles. It was fun for us to witness her mindset shift.

In the following pages, we share three sculpting tools you can use to introduce and teach this key principle to your children.

They are:

1. Failure Is Your Friend
2. Failure Is a Learning Tool
3. Try New Things

SCULPTING TOOL 1

Failure Is Your Friend

Failure is not the opposite of success, it's part of it.

Fear of failure can be the most debilitating of all human fears. But it doesn't need to be for your children as you teach them that failing, or making mistakes, is a normal part of the human experience, and that it's not only okay to fail, it can actually be a good thing.

Failure can become your children's friend.

Give them permission to make the "right" kind of mistakes, and help them understand that a mistake shows that at least they made an effort.

As former U.S. President Teddy Roosevelt so succinctly stated, "It is not the critic who counts; not the man who points out how the strong man stumbles, or where the doer of deeds could have done better.

The credit belongs to the man who is actually in the arena, whose face is marred by dust and sweat and blood; who strives valiantly; who errs, who comes up short again and again, because there is no effort without error and shortcoming; but who does actually strive to do the deeds; who knows great enthusiasms, the great devotions; who spends himself in a worthy cause; who at the best knows in the end the triumph of high achievement, and who at the worst, if he fails, at least *fails while daring greatly*, so that his place shall never be with those cold and timid souls who neither know victory or defeat."[1]

Teach your children there is a difference between failing and being a failure, and that failure is an event, not a person. Your children can learn it's not failure that prevents them from reaching their hopes and dreams; it is the *fear* of failure that prevents them from doing so.

Your children will never find their limits or their personal ceiling, unless they push themselves to failure. Remind them often: "Don't be afraid to fail!"

In other words, don't be afraid to make a mistake.

Be on the lookout for signs of perfectionism in your children. Perfectionism makes life an endless report card on ones accomplishments or appearance. It is a fast track to a long life of enduring unhappiness.

What makes it so deadly is that while those with this trait desperately desire success, they focus more of their efforts on avoiding failure. There is a substantial difference between striving for success and demanding perfection.

As American corporate trainer John C. Maxwell has said, "The greatest mistake we make is living in constant fear that we will make one."

The African impala can jump over ten feet high and more than thirty feet in distance. Yet this magnificent creature can be kept in an enclosure in any zoo with a three-foot wall. Why? Because it will not jump if it cannot see where its feet will land.

A lot of us are like this—afraid to take risks.[2] Your children will be different.

In his excellent book *How Will You Measure Your Life?*, the late Harvard Business School professor Clayton M. Christensen had this to say about children and failure:

> Encourage them to stretch—to aim for lofty goals. If they don't succeed, make sure you are there to help them learn the right lessons: that when you aim to achieve great things, it is inevitable that sometimes you're not going to make it.
>
> Urge them to pick themselves up, dust themselves off, and try again. Tell them that if they're not occasionally failing, then they're not aiming high enough. Everyone knows how to celebrate success, but you should also *celebrate failure if* it's a result of a child striving for an out-of-reach goal.[3]

Give your children the freedom to fail.

As Dr. Bob Rotella states:

> The reality is that if your dream is to accomplish something awesome, it's not going to be easy. If it were easy, everyone would be doing it. People who go for greatness are going to get knocked down a lot. They'll have difficult times. They'll struggle with doubt and uncertainty.
>
> People around them will question the wisdom of their quest. The issue is not whether you'll fail because you will. It's whether you'll get back up and keep going. It's whether you can sustain your confidence and your belief in yourself and keep bouncing back. *Failure is only final when you stop striving.*[4]

We are reminded of the story of a high school sophomore who was doing his best to find a job for the summer.

"Look here," said the office manager, "aren't you the same young man who was in here a week ago?"

"Yes, sir," said the applicant.

"I thought so. And didn't I tell you then that I wanted an older person?"

"Yes, sir," said the young man. "That's why I'm back. I'm older now."[5]

SCULPTING TOOL 2

Failure Is a Learning Tool

Failure is an excellent tutor, not a tragedy.

Failure can be a wonderful teacher if we learn the lessons it has to teach us. Teach your children that they can learn from failure by asking themselves these questions:

"What went wrong?" "What did I learn about myself?" "What can I do differently next time?" "How can this experience work for my good?"

Share with your children that failure is simply a data point and that they never really lose when they're learning something. Failure is merely a harsh word for the experience we all need in our constant quest for self-improvement.

Never a failure, always a lesson. Simply stated, failure is feedback.

It is, in fact, an integral part of any great achievement. Dave and I love to read the stories of famous failures and how the people who experienced those "failures" persisted through their early setbacks. One of our favorites is J.K. Rowling.

Rejected. Domestic abuse. Divorce. Clinical depression. These were the nightmares experienced by an out-of-work single mother living on welfare and contemplating suicide. If that person wrote a book for your kids, would you let them read it?

Seven years after she graduated from college, she saw herself as "the biggest failure" she knew. But she turned her despair into her inspiration.

"Failure meant a stripping away of the inessential. I stopped pretending to myself that I was anything other than what I was and began to direct all my energy to finishing the work that mattered to me," Rowling said in "The Fringe Benefits of Failure," a 2008 commencement speech at Harvard University.

"Had I really succeeded at anything else, I might never have found the determination to succeed in the one area where I truly belonged. I was set free because my greatest fear had been realized, and I was still alive. I still had a daughter whom I adored, and I had an old typewriter and a big idea.

And so rock bottom became a solid foundation on which I rebuilt my life."

Rowling wrote her first novel in cafés, walking from one to another, taking her daughter with her so she would tire along the way and sleep while Rowling wrote.

She pounded out her first manuscript on a manual typewriter and completed it in 1995, the year of her thirtieth birthday. Numerous publishers rejected the manuscript before the owner of a small publishing house was convinced by his eight-year-old daughter to publish the first Harry Potter book. The rest is history.[6]

Failure is not a destination, it's part of the process of getting better.

Isn't it interesting how parents get so excited when a toddler first learns to walk? They encourage their little one to take that first step, applaud loudly when they do, all the while knowing they will soon fall. Eventually the toddler learns to walk because they have fallen so many times while figuring out how to balance themselves.

But as kids get older, something interesting happens. Sometimes parents begin to discourage their kids from trying new things because they don't want them to fail—the exact opposite of when their children were toddlers and learning to walk.

Let your kids fail!

Encourage your children to "take that first step" in all areas of their lives.

We like the answers two students gave when asked, "Why are mistakes wonderful?" The first child responded, "Mistakes are wonderful because when they're made, you learn how to better yourself from the mistake.

You can approach the obstacle you made the mistake at and overcome the challenge because you learned from the mistake." The second student responded, "Anyone who hasn't made a mistake hasn't learned anything."

What kind of school produces this kind of mindset? Tom Hoerr leads New City School, a private elementary school in St. Louis, Missouri.

"One of the sayings you hear around here a great deal is, 'If our kids have graduated from here with nothing but success, then we have failed them because they haven't learned how to respond to frustration and failure.'"

Hoerr intentionally pulls kids out of their comfort zones.

"The message is that life isn't always easy," he says. His goal is to make sure "that no matter how talented students are, they hit the wall so they can learn to pick themselves up, hit the wall again and pick themselves up again, and ultimately persevere and succeed."

It is a major adjustment for everyone—especially for the parents. "It's really easy to talk about it in the abstract," Hoerr says. "Parents love the notion of resilience. They all want their kids to have it. However, no parent wants to see their kid cry."[7]

Resilience is born in the moments that humble us.

As American author Napolean Hill said, "The capacity to surmount failure without being discouraged is the chief asset of every man or woman who attains success in any calling."[8]

Learning to fall and bounce back up is in great demand in our world today. Discovering a lack of resilience among its recruits, the U.S. Army started offering the Master Resilience Training (MRT) program to fortify soldiers against the stress, demands, and hardships of military service.[9]

The following blog post was written by Levi Belnap, a Harvard Business School graduate and former business owner. It is entitled, "I'm Thankful For Failure."

> I failed and guess what? Failing is not very fun! Four months ago we shut down FindIt, the mobile app my co-founders and I poured our hearts and souls into. Today is Thanksgiving.
>
> As I reflect on my life and the roller-coaster of chasing a dream and watching it blow up in flames, I am thankful. *I'm thankful for failure.*
>
> So if failure itself felt so terrible, why am I thankful for it? Because failure forces learning. Scientists understand failure well.
>
> The scientific method is all about predicting the outcome of a certain action (hypothesis), designing an experiment to test the prediction, running an experiment, observing the outcome, learning from failures and successes, and then doing it all over again.
>
> This time tested process leads to world changing discoveries. Electricity, flight, medicine, and everything else that makes our lives so comfortable today. One that I especially love, the Dyson vacuum.
>
> James Dyson failed 5,126 times before he got it right.
>
> Each failure taught him something that led to his next experiment. Eventually the learning from each failure accumulated in the best vacuum ever built!
>
> And how do you think we got the iPhone? Did Steve Jobs' vision just magically appear in our pockets? Nope! Do you

remember the first iPod? It was big and clunky and couldn't do much compared to the iPhones we have now, but that is where the iPhone started.

One test after another, one failure after another, one improvement after another, and that my friends is how we got the iPhone. They continue to improve it today.

So why is it so easy to accept the value of failure in science and technology, but not in our own lives? I think it's because things don't have feelings, but people do. We are easily caught up in the feeling of every failure.

We worry about what other people think about us. We worry about what we think of ourselves. We are afraid to try again. Our feelings can halt our progress, but we shouldn't let them!

If I look at my failure with FindIt as a life experiment, there are some powerful observations. The worst case scenario was not as terrible as I imagined once the flames were extinguished and the dust settled.

This experience has been a pivotal moment in my life.

My hypothesis on life is that we exist to learn. The purpose of our existence is to grow and develop, to become something better than when we started. I am now convinced *failure is the path to success*, and I am starting to view my life as a series of experiments.

Tests I am running to discover what works and what doesn't in both my personal and professional lives.

So here is my prediction: Fifty years from now when I look back at my life, the failures will be the turning points that led me to happiness and satisfaction. That is why I am thankful for failure.

Now back to life, the great experiment![10]

SCULPTING TOOL 3

Try New Things

Encourage your children to try new things, to become curious discoverers. They may uncover a whole new world, interest, or passion they never knew existed. Encourage them to never be afraid to try something new.

We value what we discover more than we value what we are told.

It is better for them to lean into the stiff wind of opportunity than to simply hunker down and do nothing. As circus creator P. T. Barnum so eloquently shared in the movie *The Greatest Showman*, "Comfort is the enemy of progress."[11]

Help your children to become comfortable with being uncomfortable.

At age thirty-five, Michelangelo was invited to meet with Cardinal San Giorgio about a sculpting project. The cardinal showed Michelangelo statues from his own collection and then asked him if he felt he could create a statue worthy of inclusion.

Michelangelo answered that he thought he could and would try his best but that the Cardinal could judge for himself when it was completed. Always humble but never afraid to fail, he was ready to challenge himself against the ancient masters.[12]

Share this wise counsel that was found on a school classroom wall: "Don't decide that you can't before you discover that you can."

Sara Blakely, the founder of Spanx, shared this story about her dad:

> Growing up, my father used to ask my brother and me at the dinner table, "What did you fail at this week?" He would actually be disappointed if I didn't have something that I'd failed at.
>
> I can remember saying, "Dad, I tried out for this and I was horrible," and he would actually smile, high-five me, and say, "Congratulations, way to go!"

What it did was reframe my definition of failure.

Failure for me became *not trying* versus the outcome. And once you *redefine* that for yourself and realize that failure is just not trying, then life opens up to you in so many ways.

And my dad would encourage me any time something didn't go the way I expected it to, or if I got embarrassed by a situation, to write down where the hidden gifts were and what I learned from it.

And I started realizing in everything there was some amazing nugget that I wouldn't have wanted to pass up.

We pay a heavy price for our fear of failure. It is a powerful obstacle to growth. It assures the progressive narrowing of the personality and prevents exploration and experimentation.

There is no learning without some difficulty and fumbling. If you want to keep on learning, you must keep on risking failure—all your life. It's as simple as that.[13]

Show us a father and/or mother with a parenting approach like this, and we would love to see the kind of children produced in that type of intentional family culture.

You only fail when you stop trying.

This puts the focus on the process rather than on the outcome for your children. Something they can control (effort) versus something they cannot control (outcome). That is an empowering mindset shift.

Challenge your children to try something new every day.

As part of that, have them follow Ralph Waldo Emerson's credo: "Do what you are afraid to do." Recognize and celebrate when your child tries something new. Make it a habit to regularly ask them how they are doing with their "new" challenges.

Share with them any new things *you* have tried or are working on at the moment.

A young man was walking across campus during his first week of school at a university back east. He turned around when he felt somebody tap him on the shoulder. It was a young lady—a fellow student asking him if he would like to try out for a hip-hop dance group on campus.

She gave him a flier with details about the tryouts the next week.

Though he enjoyed dancing, he had never before been in any kind of organized dance group. However, he decided to give it a try. He made the team and thoroughly enjoyed the experience of developing new dancing skills, meeting fellow students, and performing.

One of the students he met in the group ended up becoming his business partner, and they created a company that won the business-plan competition at the university later that same year.

Over the next five years, the company grew and became number one in the United States in the online college-admissions space. It sold in November 2011 for a significant sum.

Had the young man not joined the dance group, he would have never met his future business partner or discovered a new talent and passion.

He has already learned to live his life in alignment with the following quote: "The bold don't live forever, but the cautious don't live at all. Be bold!"

A young woman heard about a new statewide TV news show for high school kids to be produced and staffed by students from around the state in conjunction with a local TV station. Even though she had no experience whatsoever, she decided to try out for an anchor position.

Her parents were proud of her for getting out of her comfort zone and making the effort, whatever the outcome might be.

She ended up being chosen, and her friends and family watched her on TV once a week throughout that school year. She thoroughly enjoyed the "stretching" experience which greatly increased her confidence.

And it all happened because she was not afraid to fail or to try something out of her comfort zone.

"I wish it would be okay if I just learned something new every OTHER day."

In other words, as a Buddhist priest once taught, "Stop being scared and just go for it. Either it will work out or it won't. That's just life."

Teach your children that in the end, they will only regret the chances they didn't take.

How Can You Encourage Your Children to Try New Things?

Children need positive experiences. Let's talk about six suggestions that will help you as a parent set the stage.

First, validate and celebrate every time your children try something new, regardless of the outcome.

Do you remember the story from chapter three about the father and daughter on the playground? If you recall, he started calling his daughter

"Tiger Tina" to help her reframe how she saw herself. This father then took it a step further in encouraging his daughter to try new and hard things.

Every time she tried something new that was hard for her, they decided to call it a "booyah" moment. The daughter would raise both hands high above her head and excitedly yell "Booyah!" every time she tried something new, whether she was successful or not.

It became a celebration of her effort, and willingness to try something new and hard. He shared with us that booyah moments have been happening in every area of her life, and her siblings are seeking out booyah moments as well.

Second, help your children develop a strong sense of independence. Let them take the lead in age-appropriate activities, like caring for themselves (choosing their clothes, getting dressed, making their own simple meals and snacks, and so on).

Third, help them experience small successes that build confidence. Celebrate small, everyday efforts with regular encouraging words, not superficial praise. Encourage your children to solve their own problems by coming up with creative solutions.

Fourth, help them feel a sense of security. You can make this happen on a daily basis by first making time for your children and then paying close attention to what they have to say. As you really listen, you validate any feelings they share.

Fifth, help your children develop resilience. They need to know they can survive life's ups and downs. They can develop a mindset of "I can do this." Help them understand that mistakes are a part of life and are fixable. When you make a mistake, own it and show your children how you figured out what to do next.

Sixth, instead of worrying about what can go wrong, your children can ask themselves, "What can go right?" "What are some potential good things that can happen if I try this?"

What are the BENEFITS of "Don't Be Afraid to Fail" for your Children?

1. They Come to Know Who They Really Are

They become comfortable in their own skin.

Annabella once met a man who'd had many successes in his youth. He was gifted with athletic skill, natural intelligence, and an outgoing personality. He graduated with honors from a prestigious university.

When he came in for therapy, this man told Annabella he had all the reasons in the world to be happy, but he wasn't. He said he had always been the star and enjoyed the praise he regularly received from others.

Yet, in spite of all his successes, he did not feel confident or comfortable with himself. His whole life, he had depended on others to make him feel good.

He needed to change the way he saw himself. Annabella taught him the necessary skills and tools, and over time, he began to see himself and his perceived flaws through a new set of eyes. He was now on the path to developing real confidence and knowing his true identity.

2. They Don't Let the Opinions of Others Affect Them

Former martial-arts champion Ronda Rousey shares her thoughts:

> The only power people have over you is the power you give them. Once you give them the power to tell you you're great, you've also given them the power to tell you you're unworthy.
>
> Once you start caring about people's opinions of you, you give up control. *"One of the greatest days of my life was when I came to understand that other people's opinions and my happiness were not related."*[14]

As someone once said, "A lion doesn't concern himself with the opinions of a sheep." Your children will become "lions" as they go through life.

3. They Become Assertive Leaders

Your children will have the inner strength to stand up for what's right. They develop the inner fortitude to say no when necessary and are assertive in their interactions with others.

As a result, they aren't bullied into bad decisions.

Individuals with deep confidence don't care about what others are doing; they are focused on what they are doing. The competition is within oneself; it's a battle of self-mastery.

Your children will become bold but respectful. They will know who they are and where they come from. They will become exemplary leaders.

4. They Naturally Develop Greater Confidence

The fact is, it doesn't matter how able or talented your children are. If they don't have confidence, it will be difficult for them to become who they are capable of becoming or develop the Masterpiece Mindset.

Confidence is earned, not bestowed.

No one can give your child confidence; they have to develop it themselves through positive experiences.

With a "Don't Be Afraid to Fail" mindset, your children develop a deep confidence in who they are, and in the positive influence they have on others. They feel no need to draw attention to themselves, to brag or highlight past accomplishments.

They are humble and teachable.

They also have no interest in putting others down. In fact, the opposite is true—they look to build others up and give others credit for their successes. They err on the side of understatement rather than exaggeration because they are comfortable in their own shoes.

5. They Become More Fearless in Their Approach to Life

Keep in mind that fearlessness is not recklessness. Being reckless is diving into something without thinking or planning. People who are fearless know what they are going to do. They set goals and have plans to execute them. They simply choose to not be afraid.

Being fearless is not the absence of fear, as fear is a normal emotion we all experience. Everybody is wired to feel fear as it is one of the body's defense mechanisms to help keep us safe. It is a warning alarm that alerts us of potential danger.

Being fearless means that you don't let your fears get in the way of what you really want to do in your life.

Fearlessness is about getting up one more time than you fall down. The more comfortable your children are with the possibility of falling down, the more resilient and fearless they will become.

Fear is interesting. There are really only two categories of fear in life: reasonable and unreasonable. One keeps us alive, while the other keeps us from truly living. Being afraid to jump out of an airplane *without* a parachute would be a reasonable fear. Jumping out of an airplane *with* a parachute would keep us alive.

Most fears, however, are unreasonable and not based on fact.

We convince ourselves that our unreasonable fears are reasonable when actually they are nothing more than an illusion in our mind. Teach your child there is a difference between the two fears and that they can convert their fears into fuel for achievement.

As French saint Joan of Arc famously said, "I am not afraid, I was born to do this."

"The greatest detractor from high performance is fear—fear that you are not prepared, fear that you are in over your head, fear that you are not worthy, and ultimately, fear of failure," said Super Bowl championship coach Pete Carroll.

"If you can eliminate that fear—not through arrogance or just wishing difficulties away, but through hard work and preparation—you will put yourself in an incredibly powerful position to take on the challenges you face.

I am a firm believer in the idea that more often than not, people will live up to the expectations you set for them."[15]

When your children choose to experience life by embracing their fears, the sky is the limit for them, and they will absolutely find their true ceiling in life. Encourage them to "experience the world, not fear it."

6. They Don't Worry about Being Perfect All the Time

Children with a "Don't Be Afraid to Fail" mindset are *unafraid* of making mistakes. They come to realize that "perfection is boring."

As Irish playwright George Bernard Shaw wrote, "A life spent making mistakes is not only more honorable but more useful than a life spent doing nothing."[16]

Ten-Second Summary

Don't Be Afraid to Fail

1. Failure Is Your Friend
2. Failure Is a Learning Tool
3. Try New Things

The purpose of this chapter is for this principle to eventually become a deeply rooted inner belief, Belief 3 (below), within the minds and hearts of your children.

This belief will reflect how they see, feel, and think about themselves and become part of their core identity. In other words, this is who **I AM.**

BELIEF 3

"I AM not afraid to fail."

OUR INVITATION

We invite you to write down your initial thoughts on teaching this critical key principle to your children. How can a "Don't Be Afraid to Fail" mindset become significant in the lives of your children? Which of the three sculpting tools stood out the most to you?

1.

2.

3.

OUR PROMISE

At the end of the day, not being afraid to fail can, in effect, create a wind behind the backs of your children as they go through life. It can create deep confidence, a more fearless mindset, and deeply entrenched resilience.

It will change their core identity and create tremendous momentum as they continue to make their way toward developing the Masterpiece Mindset.

You are Michelangelo and CAN empower your children to sculpt their lives into masterpieces!

Dave and Annabella have a video message for you that relates to this chapter. Please go to **themasterpiecemindset.com** to view it.

DO HARD THINGS

"Hardships often prepare ordinary people for an extraordinary destiny."
C. S. Lewis

A MAN WATCHED A BUTTERFLY STRUGGLE to leave its cocoon through a tiny hole. He felt sorry for it and wished to alleviate its pain, so he found a pair of scissors and snipped off the opening of the cocoon. The butterfly came out, but it was not yet a strong, healthy butterfly.

The time a butterfly spends battling its way out of its cocoon is nature's way of helping the butterfly ready its wings for flight. Sadly, the well-meaning aid the butterfly received led to its ultimate demise.

In the world of nature, hard is part of the circle of life. It is the same for your children. Doing hard things pushes, stretches, and molds your children and helps them become who they are capable of becoming.

Share with your children that if something is hard, they should strongly consider doing it. They can develop the mindset that nothing is too hard for them and that they can always try to figure out a solution to their problems and challenges.

Hard is good.

Embracing and celebrating hard things can become a critical component of your intentional family culture, and an important layer of your children's core identity.

Throughout this chapter, we will share three sculpting tools to help you introduce and teach this fourth key principle to your children. As you use them consistently, they will work together to help your children activate the immense potential contained within this principle.

The three tools are:

1. Struggle Creates Strength
2. You Can Climb the Mountain
3. You Are a Problem Solver

Sculpting Tool 1

Struggle Creates Strength

Why is it important that your children learn to do hard things? Because struggle creates strength. Strength doesn't come from winning—it comes from struggling.

The harder the struggle, the sweeter the success.

Pierre de Coubertin, founder of the International Olympic Committee, said, "The important thing in life is not triumph, but the struggle; the essential thing is not to have conquered, but to have fought well."[1]

Teach your children they need to experience the furnace of adversity to help shape them into the best version of themselves. In other words, if it doesn't challenge you, it probably won't change you.

A life spent doing hard things leads to a life of doing meaningful things.

We have never met a successful person who hasn't had to overcome numerous hard things in his or her life. Your children can come to find out that doing hard things is empowering and that nothing of value comes without being earned.

In truth, many kids today have a "microwave" mentality, wanting everything to be fast and easy! That is not adaptable for long term success in "real life."

Pain is part of the pathway to becoming who they were born to become.

When your children are coddled or overprotected, they become too dependent on you. Many parents see it backwards these days. They think struggles and failures will hurt their children's confidence, when in fact, the opposite is true.

Struggle creates true, deep confidence.

By doing hard things, your children will become more resilient and will likely experience less anxiety and depression.

As the African proverb says, "Smooth seas do not make skillful sailors."

Helen Keller, a person who knew more than just a little about struggle, said, "Character cannot be developed in ease and quiet. Only through experience of trial and suffering can the soul be strengthened, vision cleared, ambition inspired, and success achieved."[2]

Effort should always precede reward.

True confidence comes from within. The ability to regard ourselves favorably is the natural result of having accomplished something challenging. When your children say something is too hard, validate their feelings: "That does look hard." And your teaching moment has arrived!

Michelangelo came to clearly understand the value of hard things on many occasions. Here is the back story about his "invitation" from Pope Julius II to paint the ceiling of the Sistine Chapel:

> "The Holy Father is waiting for you," said his friend Giuliano da Sangallo. Michelangelo was not looking forward to the meeting because of past interactions with the pope. "I am going to favor you above all the painting masters of Italy," the pope said to him with a smile.
>
> Painting was the least of Michelangelo's art preferences, and he felt woefully unprepared and uninterested to take on such an ambitious project.
>
> "I am commissioning you to complete my Uncle Sixtus' chapel by painting the ceiling." Michelangelo was stunned, and nausea gripped him. He responded to the pope passionately, "I am a sculptor, not a painter!"
>
> The pope glowered at Michelangelo, who stood before him in a defiant pose. Their eyes met in an exchange of immovability. "Buonarroti (Michelangelo's last name), you will paint the Twelve Apostles on the ceiling of the Sistine and decorate the vault with customary designs. You are dismissed."
>
> There was nothing Michelangelo could do but submit. He kneeled and kissed the pope's ring. "It shall be as the Holy Father desires."
>
> As the meeting concluded, he turned to his friend and remarked, "Patience. We will work our way out of this predicament."
>
> The four years spent laboring on the ceiling of the Sistine Chapel would turn out to be one of the hardest and most grueling experiences of Michelangelo's life, but he took on the challenge with relish and dedication.
>
> The final result was breathtaking. It was later said of Michelangelo, "The greatest sculptor of the age suddenly revealed himself as the greatest painter of his century as well."[3]

What Can Hard Things and Struggle Do for Your Children's Brains?

Research shows that our brain is like a muscle—it changes and gets stronger when we do things that are challenging. Scientists have been able to show just how the brain grows and gets stronger when we learn.

Everyone knows that when you lift weights, your muscles get bigger and you get stronger. A person who can't lift twenty pounds when they start exercising can become strong enough to lift one hundred pounds after working out for a period of time.

That's because the muscles get larger and stronger with exercise. And when you stop exercising, your muscles shrink and you get weaker.

It is the same with our brain. When we practice and learn new things, parts of the brain actually change and enlarge, just like muscles do when we exercise them.

Inside the cortex of the brain are billions of tiny nerve cells called neurons. These nerve cells have branches connecting them to other cells in a complicated network. Communication between these brain cells is what allows us to think and solve problems.

When we learn new things, these tiny connections in the brain actually multiply and get stronger. The more we challenge our brain to learn, the more neuron connections it makes.

The result is a stronger, smarter brain. When that happens, things we once found hard or impossible—like learning to speak a foreign language or algebra—become easier.

Another thing that got scientists thinking about the brain's growth and change was babies. Even though babies cannot talk or understand language when they are born, they somehow learn to speak their parents' language in the first few years of life.

How do they do this? The key to growing the brain is practice. From the day they are born, babies hear people around them talking—all day, every day, to the baby and to each other. They have to try to make sense of these strange sounds and figure out what they mean again and again. In a way, babies exercise their brains by listening hard.[4]

At one time, our then six-year-old granddaughter Taylor struggled to complete her homework on a regular basis. She was a bright young lady, but homework was not exciting for her. Her parents asked if we'd help encourage her.

We had them bring some of her unfinished homework when she next visited us.

Dave sat down at the kitchen table with her and asked, "Tay, can you show me how well you are at doing your homework?"

She replied, "Maybe later. It's hard."

Dave then said, "*Wow, that's great that it's hard.* Do you know what hard homework does for your brain?"

She perked up and said, "No."

Dave went on. "Your brain is like a muscle. When you use it to do something hard, it actually gets stronger. The more you make it work hard, the stronger it gets. It's like lifting weights, like your daddy does. Would you like your brain to get stronger?"

"Yes!"

"Well, we'd better do this homework, then," Dave said. "I hope it's real hard." He then sat back and watched her complete her homework.

When we saw her again a few days later, Dave asked her how she was doing with her homework. When she said she was doing good, Dave asked her, "Why is hard homework good for you?"

She replied, "Because it makes my brain stronger." It was amazing how her perception of homework had changed. Hopefully it will stay that way!

SCULPTING TOOL 2

You Can Climb the Mountain

Every person who walks the earth has to learn to climb what we call the "Mountain of Hard Things." No one is exempt, especially us parents!

Children typically respond to the hard things in their lives in one of three ways:

1. Avoidance
2. Acceptance
3. Anticipation

This is what the "mountain" looks like:

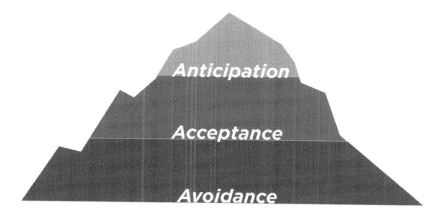

Think about where your children are right now in terms of facing the hard things in their lives. Though it is a process that takes time, they *eventually* can learn to climb to the top of the "mountain." When they get there, the view will be breathtaking!

Let's begin at the base of the mountain: **AVOIDANCE**

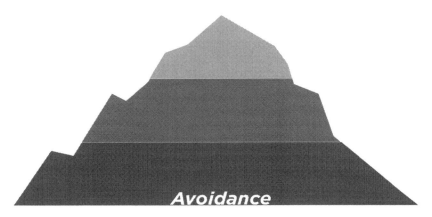

This is where your children try to avoid doing anything hard or out of their comfort zone: "I can't do it." "I won't do it." "I don't want to try." They give up easily or try to find someone else to do it for them.

If this is where your children are right now, it's perfectly okay. The beauty is that there is nowhere to go but up! They simply need successful experiences to change their mindset. Start where they are now and focus on their progress, not perfection.

In Annabella's psychotherapy practice, parents often ask what they can do to help their children not be afraid of doing hard things. Here are **ten ideas** Annabella typically shares with parents:

1. Validate and acknowledge your children's feelings: "That really does look hard."

    Children's author Dr. Haim Ginott wrote, "A child is encouraged most when he or she knows that difficulties are understood and appreciated. The best help that can be offered to them is tolerant waiting and a light comment about the difficulty of the task.

If the child succeeds, there is the satisfaction of knowing that a difficult chore was conquered. If the child fails, there is consolation that his parents knew the task was hard."[5]

2. Show support but do not overprotect.

3. Remember your children's emotional age, not just their chronological age.

4. Allow your children to try to do their best, and then provide minimal help, but let them take the lead.

5. Remember that by the time the human mind goes into the fight-or-flight response and the limbic system or "animal mind" takes over, the "thinking mind" is basically nonexistent.

   When you help your children think about possible solutions, you prevent the fight-or-flight response from automatically kicking in.

6. Do **NOT** threaten or bribe your children in order to get them to do something hard. These tactics only work temporarily.

7. Remember that every time your children believe they *need* you and you enable them, their dependence on you grows stronger.

8. Take steps to gradually remove yourself from the rescuing you tend to do.

   We once visited two of our young grandchildren who lived in San Francisco, California, and took them to a playground near their home. There was a tall teepee set up with ropes, and it looked intimidating to our then three-year-old grandson Sam.

   Dave invited him to climb it. As Sam took the first step onto the ropes, he hesitated. And then the teaching moment arrived.

   Dave first validated him by saying, "Sam, I know this looks very hard for you, and it is, but I also know you can do hard things. Hagens can do hard things, and you're a Hagen."

Our little Sam answered, "No, my daddy says I can only do easy things!" Dave and I just laughed as we knew our son would never tell him that.

Dave encouraged him, helping him climb step by step until he got to the top. Then Dave said, "See, Sam, you *can* do hard things!" Sam responded by yelling "I can do hard things!" and threw up both arms in celebration.

He was so excited. He then climbed down and proceeded to confidently climb it again on his own. It was a significant confidence-building experience for him.

We blew this picture up into a poster for his bedroom wall to help him remember his "hard" experience.

9. Tell your children you are confident in their ability: "You can do this." "There is strength in you. I can see it." If you as a parent don't believe in your children, who will? This may be the single most powerful gift you ever give to your children.

    A young man shared a story with us about his dad: "My dad would always call me 'Mr. Potential.' He saw things in me I could not see in myself. He told me he envisioned great things in my future. *I believed in his belief in me.*

    I trusted in his vision. He always told me, 'I believe in you. You can do it.' His confidence in me has gotten me through some tough times and totally changed my life."

One mother we interviewed said that her number-one goal as a mother was to do everything she could to help her children develop deep confidence in themselves.

10. What is rewarded is repeated. Recognize and celebrate each time your children make the effort to do something that is hard for them or out of their comfort zone.

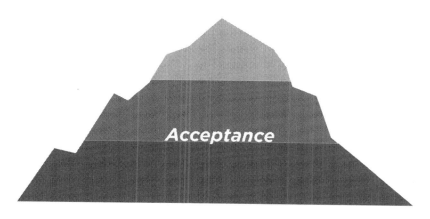

ACCEPTANCE. Your children have now made it halfway up the mountain! They are now willing to at least try hard things: "I'm willing to try." "I want to do it." "I'm not afraid to face this problem, and I think I can solve it."

Nice work, Mom and/or Dad—you are teaching them well, they are having positive experiences, and they are making excellent progress!

Remember, you can't microwave the maturity process—it takes time.

Dr. Carol S. Dweck shared a story about a high school in Chicago where students had to pass a certain number of courses to graduate. If they didn't pass a course, the grade they earned was "Not Yet."

She said, "I thought that was fantastic because if you get a failing grade, you think, *I'm nothing*, I'm nowhere. But if you get the grade '*Not Yet*,' you understand that you are on a learning curve. It gives you a path into the future."[6]

We love this approach and encourage you to share it with your children.

That experience in Chicago reminded Dr. Dweck of an earlier event in her career where she gave visual IQ tests to fifth graders and then randomly assigned what type of feedback each was given. In one group, the students were told they had performed well and were praised for their intelligence.

In the other group, the students were told they had performed well and were praised for their hard work.

Next, the children were given opportunities to practice different types of questions. The students who had been praised for their effort overwhelmingly picked harder problems than the students who had been praised for being smart.

Dweck's team then gave the fifth graders a seventh-grade IQ test; predictably, they all bombed it. But, again, the kids who had been praised for effort performed better than those who had been praised for their intelligence.

Then Dweck's team did something clever. They administered the same fifth-grade test all the children had previously aced. Again, the effort-praised children outperformed the intelligence-praised ones.

But here is the surprising thing: The kids praised for being smart actually did *worse* than they did in the first round of testing. It was almost as if they had grown less intelligent once they no longer believed they were smart.[7]

Children learn about their capabilities through their experiences, and experiences create beliefs. As a parent, you can help them process their life experiences in a more positive and emotionally healthy way.

How do you help your children keep moving up the "mountain"?

Share some of the difficulties you experienced in childhood. Make sure to indicate how those challenges changed you as a person. Share the joy you felt from accomplishing something challenging.

Help them to have a sense of curiosity and expectancy. "I wonder if I can do this." "Let's see if I can figure it out." "I wonder what I can learn from this experience."

Find ways to celebrate the moments of struggle in their lives. Help them understand that these moments of intense struggle are the moments when growth and learning are magnified. Remind them of prior successful experiences and review what they learned from those events.

"Yes, I did it, and this is what I learned."

At the dinner table or on other occasions, ask your children: "What did you do today that was hard?" Regularly reinforce to your children the value and benefits of doing hard things.

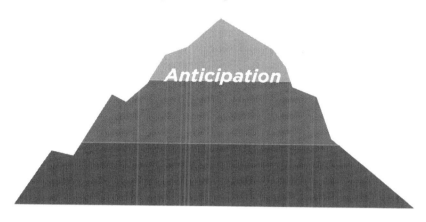

ANTICIPATION. Your children have now reached the peak of the mountain! Not only do they accept and embrace the challenge of hard things, they look forward to them. "Bring it on!" "I absolutely can do it."

"I enjoy hard things." "I want to do it." "I look forward to the challenge of hard things." They now see the "big picture" and the benefits of doing hard things in their lives.

Is this mindset really possible for your children? Yes, it is.

With this mindset, life becomes more fulfilling and enriching for your children. It allows them to *truly* find their unique potential and become the person they are capable of becoming.

They develop the mindset of attacking life rather than letting life attack them. They can then take it to another level.

Instead of just believing "I can do hard things," they develop the mindset of "I MUST do hard things to find out what my potential really is." "I need hard things to push me to find out what I am really made of." "Let me see what kind of game I really have!"

Here is an example of a "top of the mountain" mindset as shared by Dr. Dweck:

> When I was a young researcher just starting out, something happened that changed my life. I was obsessed with understanding how people cope with failures, and I decided to study it by watching how students grapple with hard problems.
>
> So I brought children one at a time to a room in their school, made them comfortable, and then gave them a series of puzzles to solve. The first ones were fairly easy, but the next ones were hard.
>
> As the students grunted, perspired, and toiled, I watched their strategies and probed what they were thinking and feeling. I expected differences among children in how they coped with the difficulty, but I saw something I never expected.
>
> Confronted with the hard puzzles, one ten-year-old boy pulled up his chair, rubbed his hands together, smacked his lips, and cried out, 'I love a challenge!'
>
> Another, sweating away on these puzzles, looked up with a pleased expression and said with authority, 'You know, I was hoping this would be informative!'
>
> "*What's wrong with them?*" I wondered. I always thought you coped with failure or you didn't cope with failure. I never thought anyone *loved* failure. Were these alien children or were they on to something?[8]

Let's do a quick recap of the "Mountain of Hard Things":

Avoidance—"I don't want to do hard things."
Acceptance—"I am willing to try hard things."
Anticipation—"I love the challenge of hard things."

SCULPTING TOOL 3

You Are a Problem Solver

One of the greatest things you can do for your children is to **NOT** do things for them.

Let them figure things out for themselves. They are more intelligent and resilient than you think. Your children can begin to develop this skill at a young age, and it can give them the confidence they need to take on more difficult problems as they grow up.

"Start by forcing yourself to stand back while your children take healthy and appropriate risks," shared one mother. "To build confidence in their world, kids have to take chances, make choices, and take responsibility for them."

Another mother shared her feelings on this subject: "I am not sitting here fifteen feet away from my kids because I am too lazy to get up and help them climb the ladder. I brought them here so they could learn to climb it by themselves. Here is my letter to you:

Dear Other Parents at the Park:

Please do not lift my daughters to the top of the ladder, especially after you have heard me tell them I wasn't going to help them. I want them to try it themselves. They're not here to be at the top of the ladder, *they are here to learn how to climb.* If they can't do it on their own, they need to figure it out.

What's more, they will have a goal and the incentive to work to achieve it. In the meantime, they can use the stairs.

I want them to tire of their own limitations and decide to push past them, and it will happen without any help from me.

It is not my job—and it is certainly not yours—to prevent my children from feeling frustration or discomfort. This is an opportunity to learn that these things are not the end of the world and can be overcome or used to their advantage.

If they get stuck, it is not my job to save them immediately. If I do, I have robbed them of the opportunity to learn to assess the situation and try to problem-solve their own way out of it.

It is not my job to keep them from falling. If I do, I have robbed them of the knowledge that falling is possible, and if they do, they can, in fact, get up again.

I don't want my daughters to learn that they can't overcome obstacles without help. I don't want them to learn that something is solved without effort. I don't want them to learn that they are entitled to the reward without having to push through whatever is necessary to earn it.

Because—and this might come as a surprise to you—none of these things are true. And if I let them think for one moment that they are, *I have failed them as a mother.*

I want my girls to know the exhilaration of overcoming fear and doubt and achieving a hard-won success. I want them to believe in their own abilities and be confident and determined in their actions.

I want them to accept their limitations until they can figure out a way past them on their own significant power. I want them to feel capable of making their own decisions, developing their own skills, and taking their own risks.

I want them to climb that ladder without any help, however well-intentioned, from you, because they can. I know it. And if I give them a little space, they will soon know it too.

So I'll thank you to stand back and let me do my job here, which consists mostly of resisting the very same impulse to hold my tongue when I want to yell, "Be careful," and choosing, deliberately, painfully, repeatedly, to stand back instead of getting involved.

Because as they grow up, the ladders will only get taller and scarier and much more difficult to climb.[9]

Teach your children that every hard thing they run away from will have power over them, and that every hard thing they go through, they conquer. That's why adversity visits the strong and stays with the weak.

Bedtime is another powerful time to deeply impact your children's mindset and inner beliefs. All kids love bedtime stories! We have never heard a child ask at bedtime, "Mom, can you show me a power point presentation?" No, it's always, "Can you tell me a story?"

Stories serve as a great vehicle for planting and nourishing ideas in your children's minds. As you lie in bed with them, consider including in your bedtime story an adventure theme with your child as the "star" who comes up with solutions to a challenging problem, doing a hard thing, etc.

Over time, they will naturally begin to see themselves as the powerful characters in your stories.

The messages from your stories can pass from their conscious minds into their subconscious minds and become permanent beliefs and part of their core identity.

The lessons will be long remembered and help them tap into their own well of inspiration.

Lastly, let your children hear your voice loving them and building them up as they close their eyes and nod off to sleep.

What are the BENEFITS of "Do Hard Things" for your children?

1. It builds confidence within them because they will have accomplished something of significance on their own.

2. It helps them develop stronger resilience.

3. It gives your children the ability to face increasingly hard things as they go through life. Eventually, no challenge will unnerve them.

4. Your children learn to enjoy the challenge of testing themselves.

5. Your children become relentless and fearless as they go through life.

TEN-SECOND SUMMARY

DO HARD THINGS

1. Struggle Creates Strength
2. You Can Climb the Mountain
3. You Are a Problem Solver

The purpose of this chapter is for this principle to eventually become a deeply rooted inner belief, Belief 4 (below), within the minds and hearts of your children.

This belief will reflect how they see, feel, and think about themselves and become part of their core identity. In other words, this is who **I AM.**

BELIEF 4

"I AM a person who can do hard things."

OUR INVITATION

We invite you to write down any ideas that came to mind that will help you integrate this principle of "Do Hard Things" into your family culture. What is your children's mindset right now toward facing hard things in their lives?

1.

2.

3.

OUR PROMISE

Learning, internalizing, and living this key principle gives your children an unbelievable advantage in life. Doing hard things will help your children become the best version of themselves and find out who they really are.

Few things in life give children more empowerment and deeper confidence than when they work hard to complete a difficult task.

Confidence comes through successful experiences, and the harder the experience, the deeper confidence they will enjoy.

Doing hard things gives your children the strength they need to continue their steady trek toward developing the Masterpiece Mindset.

You are Michelangelo and CAN empower your children to sculpt their lives into masterpieces!

ALWAYS
COMPETE

ALWAYS COMPETE

"Success comes from knowing that you did your best to become the best that you are capable of becoming."
John Wooden

DON'T BE AFRAID OF THE word *compete*. What we mean by "always compete" is that your children develop the habit of bringing their absolute best in everything they do. It's a mindset of focusing on self-improvement, and becoming the best version of themselves.

This fifth key principle will prove to be critical in your children's quest to acquire the Masterpiece Mindset, and becoming who they are capable of becoming.

Whether it is academics, sports, music, drama, chess, dance, or whatever else your children are engaged in, they bring their A game every single day. What does it *not* mean? That your children are focused solely on winning, or being "the" best.

In this chapter, we share five sculpting tools to help you introduce and teach this key principle to your children:

1. Competing Is Winning
2. Focus on the Process
3. Leverage Your Talents and Strengths
4. Find What You Love
5. School Is Cool

Sculpting Tool 1

Competing Is Winning

What does it really mean to win? Many view winning as finishing in front of someone else. They think winning is synonymous with "beating" others. The truth is that winning is not about performing better than others; rather, *it is performing to our highest ability.*

Kilian Journet, one of the most dominating endurance athletes in the world, says this: "Winning isn't about finishing in first place. It isn't about beating the others. It is about overcoming yourself. Overcoming your body, your limitations, and your fears.

Winning means surpassing yourself and turning your dreams into reality." According to this definition, you can finish a race far ahead of everyone else and still not win.[1]

Your children can play the "game of life" to win, not beat others. They can become peak performers by always striving to achieve their personal best.

By the way, this principle applies to parents as well. You can also compete to bring out the best in yourself as a parent, to become the best version of yourself.

Over time, you can eventually become the parent you are capable of becoming. Stay focused on parenting progress, not parenting perfection. You're doing just fine!

Remember, be self-aware but never self-critical!

Competition should not be about winning on the scoreboard; it should be about the process that brings out your children's highest potential. It means they are fully engaged in everything they participate in and challenge themselves to be the very best they can be.

They can compete to be a better student, a better friend, a better athlete, a better dancer, etc. This competitive mindset will lead to personal confidence, self-improvement, and empowerment in their lives.

Motivational expert Dan Clark shared the following story:

> I am paid big bucks by teams in the National Football League to work with their players to take their performance

to a higher level. When I walk into a team meeting, there are around fifty-three elite athletes who collectively represent over $100 million plus in annual salary. Totally absurd!

What would you say to them? The good news is that the same thing that motivates them is the same thing that motivates you and me: *expectations.*

At these meetings, I ask an assistant coach and a captain of the team to come to the front of the room and hold a broomstick twelve inches off the floor.

Before the meeting I get the name of the most naturally gifted athlete on the team—the guy who can jump thirty-eight+ inches high. And, for the record, every one of the thirty-two teams in the NFL has a player on their roster who can jump thirty-eight inches high!

I then ask this superstar to come forward and face the broomstick. I ask him if he thinks he can jump over the twelve-inch-high broomstick. He doesn't move and glares at me like I am out of my mind.

So I change the question: "Will you jump over this twelve-inch-high broomstick?"

Reluctantly, he hops over the bar, and this is when the teaching begins.

I ask him, "Why did you only jump twelve inches high when you and your teammates know you can jump thirty-eight inches high?"

And the answer is always the same: *"Because that is all you asked me to do."*[2]

Routinely ask your children, "How high is your bar?" "Where is your ceiling?" "How far can you go?" "I wonder how good you can become?" Help them understand that "even when you lose, you win if you've really competed."

When our oldest son turned nineteen, he went to Taiwan to do service work for our church for two years. He had to learn the Mandarin Chinese language, a difficult challenge for anybody. He spent eight weeks focused on learning the language and then was off to Taiwan.

We went to say good-bye to him at the airport. Before he got on the plane, Dave asked him if he was scared. Our son smiled and said, "Nope, it's gametime!"

In other words—referencing his basketball-playing background—it was now time for him to compete. He was looking forward to the challenge in Taiwan, even though he had no idea what to expect and could not speak the language with much proficiency.

He eventually did learn to speak Mandarin Chinese well, and the whole experience became life-changing for him.

From that point on, the term "gametime" became part of our family culture. When any of our family members face a significant challenge in their lives—a challenge that requires them to really step up and compete—we call it a "gametime" moment.

Our sons have already been in many gametime moments in their lives. This same gametime mindset can be created in your intentional family culture.

By the time Michelangelo was fourteen years old, it was already obvious that he was an enormously gifted artist. He was invited to mentor under the great sculptor Bertoldo de Giovanni.

Realizing that naturally gifted people are tempted to coast, he kept pressuring his young prodigy to work seriously at his art.

One day he came into his studio to find the young Michelangelo toying with a piece of sculpture far beneath his ability. Bertoldo grabbed a hammer, smashed the work into tiny pieces, and shouted, "Michelangelo, talent is cheap; dedication is costly!"

A friend later questioned his obsession over every detail of the Sistine Chapel ceiling, pointing out, "At that height, who will know whether it is perfect or not?" Michelangelo responded, "*I will.*"[3]

He would later say, "If there is one thing I know for sure, it's that when I hold a hammer and chisel in my hands and start, I need my full assurance that I can do no wrong. I need my complete self-respect. If I ever become content with inferior work as an artist, I'm through."[4]

Sculpting Tool 2

Focus on the Process

How do you teach your children to always compete? Learning to compete is a skill that can be developed. The secret? Teaching your children to focus only on the things they can control rather than the things they cannot control.

Control what you can control.

What does that mean? It means your children focus ONLY on the *process* and NOT on the *outcome*. The process consists of the things they can control in their lives. The outcome refers to the things they cannot control.

So, what does that look like in real life? Here are four things your children *will* always be able to control—"the processes" in their lives:

1. **Their mindset**

    In order to be successful, your children must believe that they can be successful. Their mindset will have a direct bearing on the heights they reach as they go through life.

2. **Their effort**

    Your children can control their effort level by the quality of their preparation, and by bringing their A game to everything they do. As a US Navy Seal reportedly said, "Under pressure you don't rise to the occasion, you sink to the level of your training. That's why we train so hard."

3. **Their focus on self improvement**

    Self-improvement, whether minor or major, is meaningful. All progress is a beautiful thing because baby steps and small gains really do add up over time.

    As Dr. Craig Manning says, "The biggest objective is to get better. Winning is great—we all want to win. But winning takes care of itself if we keep improving." Encourage your children to ask themselves, "How did I get better today?" "What can I do to get better tomorrow?"[5] Your children can develop a persistent commitment to self improvement.

4. Their habits

Excellence is not random. It is developed by deliberate design and achieved through incidences of excellent habits every single day. Continually remind your children that "you are what you do."

All four of these "processes" are prerequisites to any kind of achievement in your children's lives. Focusing only on the things they can control in their lives is empowering for them, and creates supreme confidence.

How can you create this mindset within your children? By looking for opportunities to recognize and celebrate their mindset, effort, focus on self improvement, and positive habits.

Behavior that is rewarded is repeated.

What are things your children will *not* be able to control—in other words, the outcome?

1. Being "the" best
2. How talented others are
3. Whether they win or lose, get the best grades, etc.

Never talk to your children in terms of absolutes. This all-or-nothing thinking leads to a focus on the wrong things (the outcome), and your children's confidence will be defined by winning or losing.

That is not a successful model for them to hang their hat on.

Life has more colors than just black and white.

Do your best to make sure that in your intentional family culture, "winning" is always about the process, not the outcome. Winning on the scoreboard becomes the icing on the cake.

In other words, do your best and forget the rest.

We met a set of parents who told us a story about their daughter's experience with winning and losing; we'll call her Melissa. She was in the fifth grade at the time and enjoyed spelling. Though Melissa had never before competed in a spelling bee, she decided to compete in her class spelling bee, and she won.

That qualified her to compete in the spelling bee for her whole school, and she worked hard studying the words in preparation. When the day of the spelling bee came, Melissa was nervous but well prepared. Her parents were there to support her.

Like every other student, she wanted badly to win.

A total of sixteen children began the competition. Melissa was able to spell all the words given to her in the first six rounds, and she and one other student became the final two spellers.

As the finalists, they would now be spelling the hardest words on the list. Unfortunately, Melissa missed the very next word. When the other finalist spelled it correctly, he was declared the winner.

The word Melissa missed was one she had studied and knew how to spell. She simply missed it. Though Melissa received a nice runner-up trophy and significant recognition for her accomplishment, she was devastated. Tears flowed for quite some time.

How could her parents help her process this "losing" experience in an emotionally healthy way? How could they reframe the experience so that it contributed to the development of positive beliefs, self-confidence, and resilience?

Here's how they handled it. They first validated her painful emotions. The loss really did hurt. They then helped her to refocus on the process and the things she had done well, rather than on the negative outcome.

It eventually became a positive experience for her in spite of the very real disappointment. These parents handled a delicate situation correctly, and their resilient daughter bounced back quickly.

She resolved to improve her spelling so she could compete in next year's spelling bee—and she eventually did.

How Does Focusing on the Things They Can Control (the Process) Build Confidence in Your Children?

First, they define for themselves what winning and losing look like.

Think about a golfer who shoots her best score ever yet loses a tournament to another golfer who played better. Is she a loser? Is she a failure? That depends on how she defines winning and losing.

When your children understand what winning really is, you will have changed their "scoreboard" for life. They now focus only on the things that really matter—the things they can control.

Second, reaching their goals becomes measurable and controllable.

Third, your children focus on self improvement rather than on trying to be perfect. Too many kids judge their progress by *the* scoreboard instead of by what they've learned or how much they've improved.

Celebrating repetition is not done often enough.

Repetition has a bad reputation and is often associated with drudgery, in fact, repetition should be celebrated as the single most powerful way the brain builds new skill circuits.

Fourth, your children's inner beliefs and confidence are tied to something they can control.

Any attempt to build confidence on external outcomes when one clearly has little or no direct control over the results eventually leads to negative experiences and negative beliefs about one's self.

Fifth, your children are more relaxed and have less anxiety while participating and competing because their minds are clear of the focus on outcomes.

Focus on outcomes leads to over-thinking. Over-thinking leads to hesitation. Hesitation leads to self-doubt, and self-doubt leads to performance struggles.

Sixth, your children develop a more fearless mindset and are able to handle pressure situations better. Teach them to practice like it matters, perform like it doesn't.

And finally, your children's journey through life becomes less anxious and stressful.

Let's next consider the experience of a ten-year-old girl who plays on a soccer team:

1. Her team has lost every game.
2. On a team of ten players, she is probably the fourth best player.
3. She has made good friends on the team.
4. The physical exercise has been good for her.

At the end of the season, she can judge the quality of her experience playing on this team in one of two ways:

1. If her focus is on only the *outcome*, or things she *cannot* control, it could be viewed as a negative experience and she might never want to play on a soccer team again. After all, her team did not win a single game, and she was not the best player.

    OR

2. If her focus is on the *process*, or things she *can* control, she could view the experience quite differently. Even though she, like everyone on her team, wanted to win every game, she could not control how good the other team was or how well her teammates would play on any given day.

Her soccer skills had improved, and she enjoyed the friendships she had made, even though her team didn't have even one victory.

Can you see how the same exact experience can be viewed in two totally different ways? It's a matter of perspective and how a "successful" experience is defined.

Do not misunderstand the principle we are attempting to teach.

This young girl wanted to win every game just as badly as anybody else. That's not all: she would like to have been the best player on the team. These are normal feelings.

We are *not* condoning or encouraging mediocrity or excusing lack of effort. She competed with everything she had. We are talking about helping her understand the realities of life and framing the experience in an emotionally healthy manner.

One father shared the counsel he gives his children, "I'm OK that you hate to lose and want to win, everybody does. But don't direct it toward other people or make excuses. Direct it to yourself by going to work and getting better so that you give yourself a chance of having a different result next time."

Your overarching teaching points can include:

- Nobody wins every game or competition.
- You won't always be the best.
- You can still enjoy the experience.
- You don't have to give up and quit.
- You can bring your best effort and feel good about it.
- There is always room for self-improvement.

In summary, process thinking versus outcome thinking is about what your children can control versus what they cannot.

Help your children to "control what they can control." In other words, "commit to the process."

The outcome becomes of secondary importance, because they know that if they honor the preparation and performance processes they've determined will work for them, the outcome will take care of itself.

They're process oriented not because they don't care about the outcome but because they know this attitude leads to the best outcome.[6]

Competition can be a positive experience for your children if handled with the proper perspective. Your children can look forward to competition as a way of measuring themselves. Competition then becomes about self improvement, about their progress, not perfection.

Competition can be about anything, from academics to athletics to music to a science fair or a spelling bee, etc. After any competition, when the time is right, parents can help their children by asking them the right question: "What could you have done to produce a better result?"

The most important thing is to encourage children to work through challenges in a problem-solving way.[7]

1-9
©2018 Bil Keane, Inc.
Dist. by King Features Synd.
www.familycircus.com

"Mommy! Guess how many slices
of bread are in a loaf!"

Competition is important because life is essentially a competition, though it's not the kind of competition where you're trying to be better than someone else. It's the kind where you're trying to be better than you thought you could be.

It's about competing against yourself, about being better than you were the day before.

Healthy competition teaches kids how to stand up for themselves, how to be vocal, and how to be comfortable getting attention. Those are skills that adapt well to life.

Here are *five ways* to encourage healthy competition in your kids:

1. Don't focus on winning.
2. Let your kids learn from failure.
3. Don't make your love conditional on their success.
4. Have fun and focus on life lessons.
5. Regularly tell them "I *love* to watch you play (or dance, etc.)."

The ability to compete is one of the defining characteristics of potential greatness. People who are *not* born to privilege or wealth can level the playing field in life by learning how to compete.

Sculpting Tool 3

Leverage Your Talents and Strengths

Every child is born with a unique combination of talents and abilities. Every one of your children has at least one gift that enables them to make their dent in the world. As a parent, you have the special opportunity to help them discover their specific gifts and talents.

A father shared this story about his son with us:

> My oldest son has no interest in athletics whatsoever. I love sports, and this has been hard for me, as I was excited

to share my love of sports with my son and watch him play. I wanted him to enjoy the camaraderie of being on a team and to learn how to compete.

I found that his natural intelligence and creativity led him to academic competitions. He recently discovered the world of robotics—of building mechanical "things" and making them work. It's all way over my head!

The beauty is that he is now on a robotic team that competes with teams from other schools. He has found his niche and he loves it. His team recently won a statewide competition and has been invited to compete at the national level.

Robotics is giving him the same benefits and life lessons he would have learned from sports. There is also scholarship money for college available! He is happy, and so am I.

As Albert Einstein reportedly said, "Everybody is a genius. But if you judge a fish by its ability to climb a tree, it will live its whole life believing that it is stupid."

Share this with your children: "Don't let the world change you. With your gifts, you were born to change the world. Don't let the world make it's mark on you. With your gifts, you were born to make a mark on the world."

Developing your children's talents and strengths should start early enough that they are exposed to different activities and interests so they can find out what they really want to invest their time and effort in.

It will take an investment of time as well as "intentional" practice for your children to develop their talents and skills to their maximum ability.

"Ignore what they don't do well," says *Shark Tank* investor Barbara Corcoran. "Instead, stay totally focused on finding what your kid does well and let them do a lot of it. They'll be better and happier for it."[8]

Encourage your children to "focus on the things you CAN do rather than on the things you CAN'T do." "Don't let what you don't have get in the way of what you do have." "Maximize what IS in you."

Sculpting Tool 4

Find What You Love

One father had this advice for his children as they were choosing their careers: "Find your passion—the one thing you like to do above everything else—and then somehow find a way to make a living at it. Do that, and the rest will fall into place.

If you do what you love, you will be willing to invest the time to become really good at it. And if you're really good at something, you'll be fairly compensated for it. With the right combination of talent, courage, and persistence, *which you have*, anything is possible for you."

That was the case with Bill Gates. As a thirteen-year-old boy in Seattle, Washington, he fell in love. Was it with a cute young lady? Nope, it was with a computer! His junior high school had time-share access to a computer, and he took full advantage of it.

He and a buddy skipped classes to work on the computer because they loved it so much, and he did odd jobs on the weekends to pay for more computer time. His mother helped him develop his burgeoning skills by organizing fundraising projects that helped pay for even more computer access.

The University of Washington also had a time-share program where, as a community service, they allowed the general public to use their computers from 3:00 a.m. to 6:00 a.m. And who do you think snuck out of his home and walked down the streets of downtown Seattle to use the computers at the university?

Bill had found his niche and purpose in life. His love of computers commanded his total focus and direction. He even dropped out of Harvard to concentrate on the creation of Microsoft Corporation.

Having spent ten years from age thirteen to age twenty-three perfecting his skills, he was once asked to estimate the amount of hours he'd spent learning how to program computers during that time. His conservative estimate was twenty thousand.

Because of this love, he was willing to pay the price to master his craft.

We recently read the story of a thirteen-year-old male ballet dancer. His mother was concerned about his posture, so she signed him up when she saw a flyer advertising a dance-technique class. It turned out to be a ballet class.

Her son was the only boy in the class, and he kept asking himself during the first class, "What am I doing here?"

But he continued to attend, and last summer he was the only boy selected to attend the Academy of Ballet. When asked about his participation, he said, "I have gotten a bit of grief about my passions, but I love being an original.

I kind of like being the odd man out. It's fun. It sets me apart from other people. It makes me feel special. People know me as the dude who does ballet." His teacher says, "He is loaded with confidence."

His father remembers a fellow parent asking how he felt about having a son who did ballet. His dad responded, "Well, how do you feel about your daughter doing ballet?" He is glad his son is following his passion and loves what he is doing.

The young man was recently photographed wearing a shirt that read, "Real men do ballet." Someone recently asked him why he chose ballet over a more traditional sport, like football.

His response? "Well, I'm the only boy in a roomful of twenty girls. Mama didn't raise no fool!"[9]

SCULPTING TOOL 5

School Is Cool

It is critical that your children develop a lifelong love of learning, and fully appreciate the relevance of education in their lives. Encourage them to be teachable, to become like sponges, always looking to absorb new information and learn new things.

Our friend's son had just started his first year of high school. In the first term, his school had all ninth graders take a career-planning class so they could start thinking about their educational futures.

As part of the class, all students had to fill out a questionnaire asking if they planned on attending college, and if they did, what colleges they would like to attend. Our friend's son stated on the questionnaire that his goal was to attend Harvard, Yale, Princeton, Stanford, or Duke.

He wanted to see if he could qualify to attend those universities, which are very difficult to get into. When the school counselor saw his answer, he approached the young man and said, "Can I meet with you after class?"

The counselor told our friend's son, "You need to be more realistic— only the very top students in America qualify to attend those colleges, but maybe if you work hard enough, you can qualify to attend Utah Valley Community College (UVCC) just down the street."

In fairness to the counselor, our friend's son did not look very smart— he wore baggy jeans and had an unconventional haircut. That's all the counselor saw. He did not know this young man personally, or the competitive fire that burned inside him.

Our friend's son came home and said to his father, "Dad, you are not going to believe what this counselor at school said to me." He recounted the story for his dad, who replied, "Get in the car. Let's go have a chat with that counselor."

They drove back to the high school and found the counselor. The father expressed his disappointment in what the counselor had told his son.

He told him, "My wife and I have spent the last fifteen years telling our son that if he works hard enough, he might be able to qualify to attend one of those colleges, and now you are telling him he can't.

You are undoing fifteen years of our encouraging words and actions. You do not know my son. You do not know what is in his mind or his heart. You do not know how smart he is or how hard he is willing to work. You have no right to take away his hope."

The counselor quickly apologized to both the father and the boy.

Three years later, our friend's son had competed hard in the classroom and was accepted to Duke University, one of the top colleges in America. He took his acceptance letter to school and found the counselor from his ninth-grade class.

He asked the counselor, "Do you remember me?"

The counselor replied, "No, I do not." The young man reminded him of the meeting with him and his dad three years earlier. At that point, the counselor said, "Oh yes of course, I do remember you now."

Our friend's son showed the counselor his acceptance letter to Duke and told him, "Please don't ever judge a student again by the way he or she looks. Do not ever underestimate their potential, their motivation, or how hard they are willing to work."

They both smiled, shook hands, and wished each other well.

Hard work and discipline contribute more to school achievement than does IQ.

As a parent, please celebrate and reward sincere effort rather than just grades. Dr. Dweck's research suggests that when parents praise effort in school rather than natural ability or intelligence, children develop a stronger work ethic and become more motivated in the classroom.

Your children will come to believe that *school is cool!* Help your children value the "process" of learning, self improvement, and work ethic, more than grades.

If their hard work results in Bs, be okay with it. In fact, if they have worked hard and received Bs, loudly and proudly celebrate their effort. A report-card grade doesn't necessarily reflect the effort a student did or didn't put into the work.

Grades are not the "be all, end all" anyway.

We all know people who were not great students in school but who have done very well in life. They simply developed other skill sets.

In addition, be careful about generalizations. Traditional schools are not a good fit for all children as some kids learn better in different environments and formats. Try and find the best educational fit for your children.

Be flexible, and most importantly, teach and model a lifetime love of learning.

What Five Things Can You Do to Help Your Children Succeed in School?

1. **Read to Your Children Often**

   Help your children develop a deep love for books. Read to them often but encourage them to read on their own as well. Regularly take them to the library so they have an unending supply of reading material.

   Reading strengthens their ability to concentrate and use their imagination—both essential life skills. Books help children travel with their minds. Children who read become adults who think.

2. **Help Your Children Establish a Clear Vision of the Benefits of Education**

   Help them understand the value of learning and education and what it can do for their future.

   We met a family who took their children on weekend trips to visit colleges up and down the East Coast. They talked to students on each campus, asking what kind of grades, test scores, and other extracurricular activities were needed to get into that particular school.

   The parents didn't care if their children ultimately went to those particular colleges or not. They simply wanted to expand their children's educational vision.

They also shared two things with them: 1) that it was possible for them as "regular" people to attend these colleges, and 2) that they would need to work very hard in school to even have a chance.

But most importantly, they let their children know that they personally believed that *it was possible* for them.

3.   Have a Consistent Family Study Time

In their intentional family culture, one family sets aside two hours—6:00 to 8:00 p.m. every evening, Monday through Friday—as their family study time. During these two hours, there are no other activities, including TV, cell phones, or video games.

If the children have no homework to do, they read books. Someone also reads books to those too young to be in school.

After the two hours of family study time are over, the kids can do whatever they want as long as they are in by curfew. The parents are with the kids during the two-hour study block and are available to help if needed. If none of the children need their help, the parents simply read on their own.[10]

In addition to establishing a consistent study time, be aware of your children's homework assignments. Create a plan for your children to take personal ownership of completing their assignments in a timely manner and actually turning them in.

4.   Take a Sincere Interest in Your Children's School Experiences

Every day after school, ask them to tell you something they learned that day. Don't allow for answers like "Nothing" or "I don't remember." Drill down and make them think. If they know you are going to ask them that question every day, they will be prepared to give you a more substantive answer.

Do your best to never miss a parent-teacher conference.

When you attend these meetings, you send your children a clear message that you genuinely care about their progress in school, and that their learning and education are important in your family culture.

We had an interesting experience with parent-teacher conferences when we moved to a new area. We wanted our children to learn how to speak Spanish—Annabella's native language—so we enrolled them in a Spanish immersion program at an elementary school in a rural area about ten miles from our home.

Our four sons were in kindergarten, second, fourth, and sixth grade at the time.

The school year started, and we noticed that none of them were bringing home any homework. When we questioned them about it, they told us they were not given any homework by their teachers.

We thought that was odd; we had never heard of a teacher or school that did not give homework.

We were curious to attend the first parent-teacher conference of the year to find out what was going on. When we got there, we asked each of our children's teachers about the lack of homework assignments.

We were basically told, "The parents in this school area have asked us not to give homework to their kids. They (the parents) said they do not have the time to monitor it or help their children with it."

They also told us that parents would not support homework or require their kids to do it.

We were shocked. In a nice way, we told the teachers we were a family that felt homework provided benefits for our kids, and that they were welcome to send it home with our children.

To their credit, each of the teachers did exactly that. Our boys weren't real thrilled with their "mean" parents, as they were the only ones in their classes required to do homework. In the end, it worked out pretty well for them.

5. **Set a Personal Example**
Your children need to see you read. They need to see your curiosity with respect to things in the world, and they need to see your love of learning.

It is better to see a sermon than hear a sermon.

As your children watch you continue to seek out opportunities to learn new things, they will realize, as author Annabel Monaghan did, that "The truly educated never graduate."[11]

What you *do* is much more powerful than what you *say*.

What are the BENEFITS of "Always Compete" for your children?

1. It is something in life they can control.
2. It gives them a greater sense of confidence and empowerment.
3. They become unafraid of uncomfortable (new) situations.
4. They find more enjoyment and engagement in their activities.
5. They become more fearless in pursuit of their hopes and dreams.
6. They learn to love learning and competing in the classroom.

Ten-Second Summary

Always Compete

1. Competing Is Winning
2. Focus on the Process
3. Leverage Your Talents and Strengths
4. Find What You Love
5. School Is Cool

The purpose of this chapter is for this principle to eventually become a deeply rooted inner belief, Belief 5 (below), within the minds and hearts of your children.

This belief will reflect how they see, feel, and think about themselves and become part of their core identity. In other words, this is who **I AM.**

BELIEF 5

"I AM a person who competes in everything I do."

OUR INVITATION

We invite you to consider what stood out in this "Always Compete" chapter and record it below. How can you introduce in an intentional way the sculpting tools included in this principle? Any thoughts on possible ways to teach your children about focusing on the process?

1.

2.

3.

OUR PROMISE

Learning to always compete in everything they do can become an incredibly powerful mindset for your children and keep them on track to developing the Masterpiece Mindset.

Your children can learn what "winning" really means: to compete and always strive to be their best.

They learn to focus only on the process—on the things they can control in their lives. Really "competing" *is* winning, and this mindset can become a featured component of your intentional family culture, as well as a necessary part of your children's core identity.

You are Michelangelo and CAN empower your children to sculpt their lives into masterpieces!

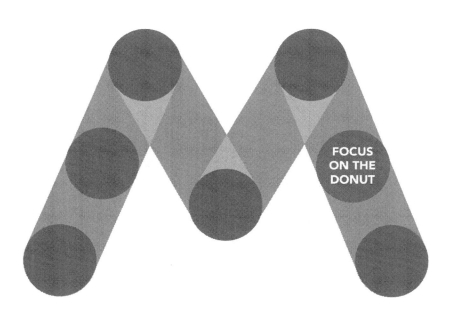

FOCUS ON THE DONUT

"Gratitude is not only the greatest of all virtues,
but the parent of all the others."
Cicero

YOUR CHILDREN (AND MAYBE YOU) probably love Krispy Kreme donuts. We sure do! When your children are getting ready to take that first bite, do you think they focus on the donut or the hole in the middle?

We don't know about you, but we don't even see the hole as we anticipate that first sugary bite, especially if it has been warmed up!

This sixth key principle is about teaching children to be grateful for what they *do* have (the donut) in their lives, rather than what they *don't* (the "hole").

Unfortunately, many people go through life focusing on the hole rather than the donut. Teach your children to be different—to focus on being grateful for what they have rather than on what they don't have.

Gratitude is the secret sauce of happiness.

Gratitude softens hearts and will become an important component of your children's core identity. You can plant these seeds from an early age, and an attitude of gratitude can become a lifelong, deeply held belief for your children.

In this chapter, we share four sculpting tools you can use to introduce and teach this key principle to your children:

1. Know Who You Are
2. Never Forget the Shoulders You Stand On
3. Run Your Own Race
4. Appreciate What You Have

SCULPTING TOOL 1

Know Who You Are

Encourage your children to be grateful for who they are, and to embrace and celebrate their uniqueness. Children who are grateful for who they are learn to *own* who they are.

When they own who they are, they become secure with who they are.

They realize that how others see them is not nearly as important as how they see themselves.

"I Define Myself, and I Know Who I Am."

How do your children really see themselves? Whatever is on the inside eventually shows up on the outside.

It's vital that they develop an empowering core identity. "This is who **I AM**."

This deeply rooted core identity gives them the needed confidence they need to walk in their own shoes and express their own voice as they go through life.

The greatest love of all is learning to love yourself.

As American essayist Ralph Waldo Emerson once said, "To be yourself in a world that is constantly trying to make you something else is the greatest accomplishment." That is certainly a mentality that should be encouraged, applauded, and celebrated in your children.

Their identity will determine in large measure their destiny. If your children do not correctly understand their identity, they can never correctly understand their potential destiny.

As they come to understand their true identity, their vision, confidence, and motivation will be greatly expanded and heightened.

When you feel that they are ready, have each of your children complete this sentence: "**I AM**_____." Whatever follows these two words determines what kind of life they will live and who and what they can become.

These "**I AM**" descriptions of themselves should be written with directness and can include a vision of their future possibilities. They are, in essence, identifying their core identity and how they see themselves at that point in time.

Encourage them to regularly revisit and add to their "**I AM**" list.

Here are some examples: *I AM* honest. *I AM* a good person. *I AM* a hard worker. *I AM* a person who sees the good in others. *I AM* fearless. *I AM* the source of my own happiness. *I AM* important because I belong to a family that loves me. *I AM* one of a kind. I like who *I AM*. *I AM* grateful for the things I have, etc.

"I just want to be me." "Who was I born to be?" "What was I born to do?" "Who am I capable of becoming?"

Hopefully, each of the seven beliefs will eventually appear on their "**I AM**" list as they become permanent, deeply-anchored beliefs in your children's minds.

The opinions your children have of themselves will become the *most important* opinion they will ever have.

How can you teach positive "identity" to your children?

Let's look at the way the Covey family did it. Stephen M. R. Covey's father was Stephen R. Covey, author of international best seller *The 7 Habits of Highly Effective People*.

Within their family culture, Stephen R. Covey used a fascinating analogy to teach his nine children this concept: "My father always talked about the idea of the '*social mirror*.'

He said the social mirror is kind of like the carnival mirrors in the crazy house at circuses or amusement parks that distort reality," Stephen explained. "They make you look like somebody else.

We all laughed because we knew it was not a true reflection of what we really look like.

He would tell us kids, 'Don't see yourself through social mirrors or how others see you. Instead, see yourself in the "*divine mirror*," which is how God sees you—and how your parents and other people who believe in you see you.'

It was my dad's way of giving us a vision of who we really were, and it created real confidence in us."[1]

In his book *The Divine Center*, Stephen's father stated it this way: "Now consider what happens when the basic source of a person's definition of himself is the social mirror—that is, the reflection of how other people perceive him.

He has no true reference point to compare with this social mirror. He thinks that the social reflection is his *real self*. He internalizes this view into a self-description or self-image or self-concept. It becomes his label. He believes it and accepts it." [2]

As your children learn to "see" themselves through the correct mirrors, they come to see themselves for who they really are and who they can become. As this happens, they begin to develop a lifelong empowering core identity for themselves.

This issue is a huge challenge for today's parents in our Instagram, Facebook, Twitter, Snapchat, and YouTube culture, where children often define themselves by social media.

Children are fooled into thinking that these social mirrors reflect their real selves, and they lose perspective and gratitude for who they really are. When this happens, their confidence erodes, and increased anxiety, depression, and suicidal thoughts kick in.

Real confidence is not "They like me," but "I'm fine if they don't."

We live in a world of comparison. Social media has made this worse as we go online and compare our seemingly less exciting lives with the "fake lives" we see from others. Many of these fake lives are edited, boastful and unreal.

Some children (and parents) have unrealistic expectations that they should be happy all the time, and if they are not, they feel like something is wrong with them.

Social media has been sold to us as a way to improve our *connection* with one another. Instead it has evolved into a *comparison* with one another. Connection or comparison—what will it be in your home?

Comparison is the thief of joy.

Help your children understand that most social media posts are "highlight reels" of people's lives and not reality. The social mirror is so pervasive today that parents need to closely monitor the mirrors their children are using to define themselves.

Teach them that: "You don't have to be like anybody to be somebody."

Over the Christmas holidays, my son and his family who were living in London at the time, came to visit Annabella and me. While they were here, we went out one evening for dinner.

While I was in line to get food with my daughter-in-law, a young woman who was also in line, said to her, "Hi Rachel!" My daughter-in-law did not know her. "Hi, do I know you?" The woman responded, "No, you don't know me, but I know you. I'm one of your Instagram followers."

Because my son and his family had been living in London for four years, they were able to do quite a bit of traveling throughout Europe as it is inexpensive to do so, and they documented their family adventures on Instagram.

Somehow this woman had found them online.

When my daughter-in-law told the woman that they were moving back to the United States in the spring, she responded, "No, you can't do that. I live my life through you!" My daughter-in-law laughed awkwardly.

We ordered our food and said goodbye to the woman. The sad thing is that I'm not sure if the young woman was joking or not.

Share with your children that when they look for the approval of others, they inadvertently allow the thoughts of others to become their own. Teach them, "The less you care about what other people think about you, the happier you'll be."

Social media is also dangerous for your children as they can be exposed to things (or people) they are not emotionally ready to handle.

Parents often ask, "At what age is it safe to give my child a cell phone?" The answer is "At what age do you want your child to become an adult?" Think about that for a moment.

It's like giving your children a snake. They will eventually get bitten. Strive to set a good social media example for your kids.

In a 2016 survey by Common Sense Media of 1,800 parents, 56 percent of parents said they are concerned that their children may become addicted to technology.

Yet in the same survey, researchers found that parents themselves spend more than nine hours a day in front of the screen, with almost eight hours of that time focused on personal social media.

The survey also revealed that despite that huge amount of time spent online, *78 percent of all parents* believe they are good technology role models for their children.[3]

Miranda Lambert is one of the top performers in the country music world. At the 2015 Country Music Awards show, she was selected as Female Vocalist of the Year. She also won in the Song of the Year and Album of the Year categories. But being on top was not always the case for her.

As a young girl, Lambert was briefly homeless when her parents' private investigation business failed in the economic collapse resulting from the 1980s Texas oil bust. They had to start over, so they moved in with an uncle who was a goat farmer.

"After we got back on our feet, we had a subsistence farm where we literally lived off the land," Miranda explains. The farm yielded rabbits and chickens for the table, while her mother's garden provided fresh produce.

"My mom would say, 'Go out to the garden and get what you want for dinner,' and she would make things like rabbit stir-fry. It was good," Miranda says, "but when you are a kid, you say, 'I just want Burger King.'"

Miranda credits her mom with the best advice she's ever received: "Know who you are and stick with it." And that applies to music, business, relationships, personal style, and everything else, she says.

"In the music industry, I think sometimes artists are pushed in a direction that might be popular, but it's not the song or message they want to send as a human being," Miranda says. "When someone told me to change a lyric or wear this, that just wasn't an option for me.

My biggest advice to anyone: *If you don't know who you are, how is anyone else supposed to know?*"[4]

Sculpting Tool 2

Never Forget the Shoulders You Stand On

Another way for your children to figure out and remember who they are is to know their family roots and family story. "Remember who you are and where you came from."

What is your family story? Have you shared it with your children? Having a knowledge and understanding of where they come from gives children a real sense of confidence and identity: "I belong to this family."

Share with your children that they are "standing on the shoulders" of family members who have gone before them. Share stories from your family history that help them get to know their grandparents and great-grandparents, aunts and uncles etc.

Everyone deserves to be remembered, and every person, no matter how seemingly ordinary, has had extraordinary experiences. Your children (especially when they are young) will love to hear about them.

As you share stories about both their struggles and successes, they can become proud of who they are and where they come from. Learning about family stories together with our children helps us to connect. It bonds our relationships in the present, as well as to the past.

Dave's family tree extends back to Norway and Ireland. One thing our sons have gotten a real kick out of is hearing that some of their ancestors were Irish rebels. They know that the blood of these ancestors runs through them and is part of their DNA.

There can be great power in a family name, and it can become an inspirational force for good in the lives of your children. Teach your children to be proud of their name and to embrace the opportunity of representing it well: "I come from a great heritage and have a great name."

Teach them to embrace any expectations that come with their name. They are still individuals, but their name is also part of giving them vision: "This is who we are as a family."

A family we interviewed had this to say about their name: "What a great stewardship I have with my family name."

They created a family-history book of their ancestors going back many generations. At a recent family reunion, each member of the family (including all the children) was assigned to do a report on an ancestor.

Each person presented his or her report to the entire extended family, and their reports were included in a family history book for future reference. It became a special experience for the whole family and gave them a deeper feel and love for who they really were, and what great stock they came from.

Stories are an excellent agent for helping to define your family and for teaching your children, "This is what we believe in as a family." You may consider creating a family bucket-list item to plan a trip where your ancestors once lived.

Walk where they walked, and help your children feel and understand where they come from and who they really are.

One of our sons recently did just that with his wife and three daughters (seven-year-old twins and a four year old) when they visited Ireland and went to some cities where some of our ancestors once lived.

After doing research and visiting graveyards, they found the gravestones of a set of great-great-grandparents on my mother's side behind a big bush. They were ecstatic!

Our son Brad and his girls in Ireland.

The importance of family roots is backed by some interesting research by Dr. Marshall Duke, a psychologist at Emory University, and his wife, Sara, also a psychologist.

Sara had noticed something about her students. "The ones who know a lot about their families tend to do better when they face challenges," she said. Her husband was intrigued and set out to test the hypothesis.

The two developed a measure called the "Do You Know?" scale, which asked children to answer twenty questions.

Examples included "Do you know where your grandparents grew up?" "Do you know where your mom and dad went to high school?" "Do you know where your parents met?" "Do you know an illness or something really terrible that happened in your family?" "Do you know the story of your birth?"

Dr. Duke and his colleagues asked these questions of about four dozen families in the summer of 2001 and taped several of their dinner-table conversations. They then compared the children's results to a battery of psychological tests the children had taken.

He reached an overwhelming conclusion: the more children knew about their family history, the stronger their sense of control over their lives, the higher their level of confidence, and the more successfully they believed their families functioned.

The "Do You Know?" scale turned out to be the best single predictor of children's emotional health.[5]

SCULPTING TOOL 3

Run Your Own Race

Jared Ward is a former college All-American track star. In 2016, he decided to try to qualify for the U.S. Olympic team in the marathon race. During the Olympic Trials he had a race plan, but during the race it appeared the leaders might pull away from him, and he briefly thought about abandoning his plan.

He ultimately decided to "run his own race, not somebody else's," the one his body needed, and the one that gave him the best chance to make his first Olympic team. It worked. He made the team that went to Rio de Janeiro, Brazil, and shocked most people with a top 10 finish.

Your children can learn to run their own race as they go through life.

Hou Yifan's favorite chess piece is not the mighty Queen but the humble pawn. "When the pawn gets to the other side of the board, it can become anything except the king," says the woman who at fourteen became the game's youngest female grandmaster, and at sixteen its youngest women's world champion.

"To me it shows that regardless of your background, if you stick to your goals and your process, eventually you can become a better version of yourself."[6]

Encourage your children to "become the best version of yourself, not someone else." Teach them that "God made you to be you, not someone else."

Hou, now twenty-four, remains the world's greatest female chess player—she has won multiple world titles since graduating from high school. For her, the best way to live life is to focus on your own self-improvement. "You have to be the hero of yourself."

Consistently teach your children to focus on self-improvement, on getting better, on progress, not perfection. Teach your children to strive to become the best version of themselves.

Life for your kids should be about becoming, about becoming "their" best, not "the" best. How does one do that? One small step at a time, continuing to move, however slow, forward.

If they are struggling, remind them that "it's never too late to become who you are capable of becoming."

And finally, encourage them: "Run your *own* race, at your *own* pace."

SCULPTING TOOL 4

Appreciate What You Have

Ingratitude leads to entitlement.

Entitlement behavior is a major concern for most parents. No parent deliberately sets out to raise kids who are spoiled, lazy, or entitled.

9-26
© 2015 Bil Keane, Inc.
Dist. by King Features Synd.
www.familycircus.com

"This tastes like water from the
bathroom. Mommy always gets
my water from the kitchen."

Many of today's children have the idea that:

- I don't have to work for something.
- I want that, and I want it right now!
- Because everyone gets a ribbon, medal, or trophy just for participating, that is how real life works.
- I should receive an A for just showing up to class.
- Everyone is special *before* they do anything special.

As Florida State University professor Dr. Roy F. Baumeister said:

> This *supposed* promotion of self-esteem doesn't actually foster healthy self-esteem in kids. It just gives them the message that rewards are meaningless and they are entitled to be treated well regardless of what they do.

That's not a good message to learn, and it's *not adaptive* for life.

Problems occur when children are told they are great no matter what they do—because the parents are afraid that they'll damage their kids' self-esteem if they point out what they did is bad.

That approach is what creates narcissism.[7]

A recent study published in the *Journal of Consumer Research* found that some parenting behaviors and tactics actually make a child more materialistic as the child becomes an adult.

Researchers surveyed more than seven hundred adults about their childhood circumstances, relationships with parents, and the types of discipline they received as children.

According to Boston Globe Media, the researchers concluded that there are three parenting behaviors that especially lead to an increase in materialism: rewarding a child's accomplishments by giving them gifts; showing affection with material items; or punishing a child by taking away one of their possessions, such as a favorite toy.

The researchers explained that when parents use material items as rewards or punishments, "kids are more likely to judge their own success and the success of other people in their lives by the kinds of possessions they own."

Lan Chaplin, an associate professor in marketing at the University of Illinois–Chicago who assisted in the study, suggested that parents should use material items in moderation.

"Each time children express their gratitude, they become more aware of how fortunate they are, which paves the way for them to be more generous and less materialistic," Chaplin adds. "Spend time with your children and model gratitude and generosity to help curb materialism."[8]

So what can you do as a parent to curb potential entitlement behavior with your children?

Consider these three *R*s:

1. Resources
2. Responsibility
3. Reality

When you provide resources, you also need to provide responsibility. For example, you say to your son or daughter, "You can use the family car (resource) tonight as long as you fill it with gas (responsibility)."

Children who receive excessive resources with little or no responsibility become entitled.

What about the reality part? Children need to understand where the family resources come from and how much effort it takes to create them. They need to be taught the value of a dollar.

Being able to connect a sum of money with what it takes to earn that money helps children develop a clearer understanding of its value.

Teach your children there is no proverbial "money tree" in the backyard and that Mom and/or Dad work very hard to provide the resources the family has. In other words, responsibility (work) creates resources.

If they would like to have more resources, the reality is that they need to do more work. One dad we interviewed makes it a habit to pick up pennies he sees on the ground in parking lots and on sidewalks.

His children once asked him why he picked them up, since it was only a penny.

His response? "A penny is valuable. Pennies become nickels, nickels become dimes, dimes become quarters, and quarters become dollars. Dollars buy things our family needs."

In a simple way, he is teaching his children the value of a dollar.

Resources + Responsibility + Reality = Reduced Sense of Entitlement

Here are a few suggestions to help you reduce potential entitlement in your children:

First, set a good example.

Remember, it is better for your children to see a sermon than hear a sermon.

Teach and show your children the difference between wants and needs. Just because you can afford it doesn't mean you have to buy it.

A popular quote attributed to the Indian poet Rajinikanth says:

> Whether you have a Maruti or a BMW, the road remains the same. Whether you travel economy class or business, your destination doesn't change. Whether you have a Titan or a Rolex, the time is the same. Whether you have a Samsung or Apple iPhone, the people who call you remain the same.
>
> There is nothing wrong with dreaming of a luxurious life. What needs to be taken care of is to not let the *need* become *greed*. Because needs can always be met, but greed can never be fulfilled.

Second, make work an important part of your family culture.

Work fosters ownership and responsibility. Do work projects with your children at home; they will find great satisfaction in challenging projects, and completing something hard builds confidence and resilience.

Here's an inspiring story from an intuitive father:

> The exterior woodwork of our home was in need of redecoration. I cleaned and prepared the surface and applied an undercoat. In my mind, I could visualize the flawless gloss finish that would be a byproduct of my labors.
>
> Our five-year-old son, Kevin, watched as I prepared to apply the final gloss covering. He asked me if he could help me. I hesitated before responding, considering what effect this would have on the fulfillment of my dream.

Alternatively, how would he feel if I declined his offer? It was almost as if I heard someone else say, "*That would be a great help, Kevin. Thank you!*"

Providing him with an old shirt of mine that covered him completely—it almost touched the floor and the sleeves were rolled back several times—we went to work on the door that secured the main entrance to our home.

Kevin applied paint to the bottom panel as I worked on the top section. I noticed that because of his age and physical stature, he wasn't able to spread the paint evenly and that beads of paint were forming.

Each time he bent down to recharge his brush, I hastily smoothed out the paint on the bottom panel, returning to my assigned area quickly so he would not realize what I was doing.

After a while, I decided that *more important* than a first-class paint job was the opportunity to work with my son.

On reflection, I realized how well he was doing. Thereafter, every time I approached the door and I saw the distinctive style of decoration, I was reminded of what is most important in my life.[9]

Please share with your children the necessity and beauty of work. A part-time job in high school and college should be strongly considered, especially during the summer months.

Work brings a sense of dignity and accomplishment.

Someone once said, "Flipping burgers is not beneath your dignity. Your grandparents had a different word for burger-flipping: *opportunity*."

When you earn it, you own it.

Help your children develop an "earn everything" mentality. When you "earn everything," it means it's yours. You own it. Nothing is going to be given to you. When you own it, you fight for it, you'll protect it, and you'll do more.

In a survey of 1,001 U.S. adults by Braun Research, 82 percent reported having regular chores growing up, but only 28 percent said they now require their children to have them. Decades of studies show the benefit of chores for children—academically, emotionally, and even professionally.[10]

Children can have chores assigned to them from an early age. They should get their allowances based on how well they perform their chores for the week. There should be no "something for nothing" allowances.

What are the benefits of "pay for performance" allowances?

1. They demonstrate that money comes from effort and execution.
2. They create a personal perspective on the value of money.
3. They help your children develop responsibility.
4. They are a springboard to other beneficial financial lessons.

One family we interviewed said, "Jobs were assigned every Saturday morning in our home to each of our children. They would receive their 'allowance' if the jobs were 'done right and done well.' Dad was the inspector."

This same family had kitchen assignments every evening after dinner. There was no pay attached to these chores. Each child had a cleanup assignment, whether it was clearing the dinner table, stacking the dishwasher, putting away the uneaten food, or washing counters alongside their dad, who was working at the sink.

If any of them complained, they were given an additional job. He often joked with his wife, "I am probably the only Fortune 500 CEO in America with dishwater hands!"

One set of intuitive parents we interviewed provided their children with a way to earn extra money in addition to the allowance they earned for doing assigned chores. They gave their children a list of books they could read.

This list contained inspirational books as well as biographies of accomplished individuals. To earn the "extra allowance," the children had to put together a detailed book report that was reviewed and approved by the parents.

If children want extra money, they should have to work for it. When your children decide they really want something, they should work to pay for at least part of it.

"I've decided I don't have to be a billionaire. Just a millionaire will be fine with me."

Help your children find creative work opportunities. A single mother shared her story about when her family moved to a new area. The kids were eleven, nine, and seven years old at the time and lived close to some college student apartments.

They wanted to buy video games, but the small allowance they earned for their chores was not enough for them to buy even one game, so they decided to go out and knock on the students' apartment doors and ask if they would like their trash taken out for twenty-five cents.

They did the same thing week after week. Some of the students were so impressed with the children's initiative they gave them extra money. Their mother was pleased to see her children's motivation and how they had come up with their own idea to make money for things that were important to them.

As they bought their own video games, they felt a great sense of ownership, pride, and responsibility. They also developed confidence and entrepreneurial skills.

Third, spend time with your children instead of spending excessive money on them. As Abigail Van Buren—the famous "Dear Abby" newspaper columnist—wrote, "If you want your children to turn out well, spend twice as much time with them and half as much money."

Don't allow your children to play the comparison game when it comes to the things they have versus what others have.

Fourth, point out role models who are living their lives in alignment with this principle.

Fifth, point out examples of entitlement behavior so your children learn by contrast.

One father shared a story about one of his sons who had just completed graduate school and was interviewing for a job. He asked his dad if he should negotiate for an up-front signing bonus and other extra benefits like the other candidates were.

His older brothers were encouraging him to do exactly that. His dad suggested he ask himself one question when they made him an offer: "Is it fair?" If the answer was yes, he should take the job and not be greedy in his negotiations.

The dad counseled him that asking for the extras would send the wrong message to his new employer. He further told his son that he should first go to work and create value for the company and then negotiate for more salary after he proved himself valuable.

He shared with his son that dollars typically follow value. The son ignored his brothers' suggestions, followed his dad's advice, and took the offer without further negotiations.

His boss later told him how much he respected him because of the way he'd conducted himself up-front. He has been given subsequent promotions because of the value he has created for the company and the initial relationship he was able to forge with his boss.

Be a parent to your children, not their best buddy.

Always maintain the parent-child respect level. You can have a close relationship with your children, but they do not need to love you every minute. Your kids will get over the disappointment, but they won't get over the effects of being spoiled.

So don't be hesitant to tell them "No" or "Not right now," and let them fight for what they value the most.

One mother told us, "Don't let the tail wag the dog. You are the parent. Be strong. Say no when you have to, and then follow through. Let your children experience the consequences of not doing what you have asked them to do.

Don't let them slide with keeping their rooms clean or doing their work assignments around the house. *We have noticed that typically stricter parents have better results.*" And then the father weighed in: "Kids need limits; they are begging for limits. Give them limits."[11]

How Can You Teach Your Children to Be Grateful?

1. Model the desired behavior. Regularly share with them what you are grateful for.

2. Ask your children each day to tell you at least one thing they are grateful for and why.

3. Make gratitude a defined feature of your intentional family culture. The grass isn't always greener over there; it's greener where you water it.

4. Help your children notice and appreciate the little things in life.

5. Encourage your children to find opportunities to simply say "Thank you."

What are the BENEFITS of "Focus on the Donut" for your children?

1. They become grateful for who they are and what they have.
2. They come to know who they really are and where they come from.

3. They do not allow themselves to be defined by social media.
4. They strive to become the best version of themselves.
5. They do not become entitled.

TEN-SECOND SUMMARY

FOCUS ON THE DONUT

1. Know Who You Are
2. Never Forget the Shoulders You Stand On
3. Run Your Own Race
4. Appreciate What You Have

The purpose of this chapter is for this principle to eventually become a deeply rooted inner belief, Belief 6 (below), within the minds and hearts of your children.

This belief will reflect how they see, feel, and think about themselves and become part of their core identity. In other words, this is who **I AM.**

BELIEF 6

"I AM grateful for who I am and what I have."

OUR INVITATION

We invite you to think about how implementing and living "Focus on the Donut" in your intentional family culture can change the quality of your children's lives. Is there a specific sculpting tool you think you need to focus on right now? Record your thoughts below:

1.

2.

3.

OUR PROMISE

"Focus on the Donut" is a life-enhancing belief for children, bringing needed balance to their lives. It softens their heart, reduces sense of entitlement, and becomes a significant layer of their core identity.

In addition, it moves them all-the-more closer to developing the Masterpiece Mindset and becoming who they are capable of becoming.

You are Michelangelo and CAN empower your children to sculpt their lives into masterpieces!

Our final key principle is coming up in the next chapter. Any ideas as of what it could be?

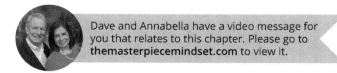

Dave and Annabella have a video message for you that relates to this chapter. Please go to themasterpiecemindset.com to view it.

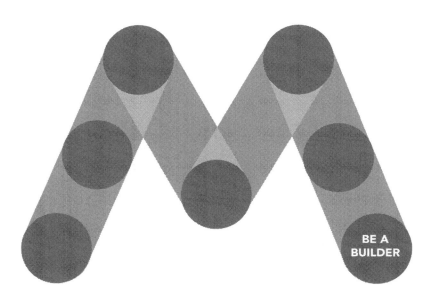

BE A BUILDER

"Try not to become a person of success, rather become a person of value."
Albert Einstein

B E A BUILDER" COULD BE the most significant key principle your children ever learn to internalize and live. What does it mean to be a builder? It simply means your children look for ways to build up other people.

As they build others at home, school, and in their community, they also build themselves. Builders of people become leaders of people. Your children can ask themselves, "Who needs me today?" "Who can I build up today?"

This seventh and final key principle reminds your children, "Life isn't just about you. It's also about bringing out the best in other people." It turns your children's focus from themselves to others and creates a healthy balance in their lives.

They can become instruments in God's hands as they bless and lift others. Most importantly, this principle softens their hearts and brings them one step closer to the Masterpiece Mindset.

In this chapter, we share three sculpting tools to help you introduce and teach this key principle to your children.

They are:

1. Sharing Is Caring
2. Choose Kindness
3. Create Value

SCULPTING TOOL 1

Sharing Is Caring

Your children look for opportunities to build others by being generous with their time, talents, and treasure. Help your children internalize that it is a privilege to be able to use what they have to lift others.

Routinely ask them, "What did you do to build someone up today?"

They then become part of the solution rather than the problem as they go through life.

Generosity can become a hallmark of your intentional family culture, and an important layer of your children's core identity. The secret to happy living is giving.

A father we interviewed weighed in on this subject:

> We have tried to teach our children the concept that "where much is given, much is required." That we are stewards and that we have a responsibility to give back. That the gifts that we have been given are to serve other people.
>
> That our gifts give us a platform to do good, and that is the purpose of the gift—whether the gift be money or other special talents. This has been helpful for us as parents, though it is still a struggle sometimes because of their friends.

Wise counsel: "Seek to bless, not impress."

Kids have an amazing ability to find service opportunities despite the fact that they generally have limited means. The scope of the service is not what makes the difference. It is the service they render that makes all the difference.

Or to put it in perspective as Dalai Lai said, "If you think you are too small to make a difference, try sleeping with a mosquito."

Zack Francom was a first grader when his school challenged all the students to raise money to buy wheelchairs for people who could not afford them. The first year, Zack's goal was to make enough money to buy one wheelchair, which cost eighty-six dollars.

He opened a cookie stand in front of his house and was successful in meeting his goal.

After his success the first year, Zack decided to raise his sights. In his fourth year, "Zack's Shack" has raised enough funds to purchase 293 wheelchairs. In total, Zack raised over $85,000 for the purchase of wheelchairs!

The project has become a family affair. His mother and grandmothers help him with the baking, and his dad helps with the business end. Zack recently passed the project on to his six-year-old sister, Helen, and it's now called "Helen's Hut."[1]

With a goal of $500, seven-year-old Cheyanne Prather was on a mission to raise money and buy clothes for the homeless in her city. The second grader asked her mother to take her to the store to buy candy. Her mother was surprised when Cheyanne told her the candy wasn't for her but was part of her plan to help others.

With about forty dollars in allowance earned from her grandfather, she bought posters, juice boxes, and treats and then set up shop outside her brother's home. She also sold treats on the sidewalk of Center Street in her hometown.

"I haven't paid for any of this," said her mother. "This is all her." Though customers were plentiful on Center Street, she saw the most success when she sold treats at a local high school football game. After several weeks of fundraising, Cheyanne made a total of $556.

Using discounts provided by the local JCPenney store, she used the money to buy clothes for kids in need. She then delivered the clothes to a local homeless shelter in her community. "For a little girl, $500 is a lot of money," said her mother.

"The experience reminded us that even if you don't have a lot, you can give because someone else has less."[2]

And one final example. Four high school students at Boca Raton Community High School in Florida decided to make a difference in the lives of their fellow students. There are 3,400 students at their high school, and it is said you can go years without seeing the same student twice.

When they noticed that many students ate lunch by themselves and appeared to be isolated from their peers, they decided to start a group called "We Dine Together" with the goal that no one at their school should have to eat alone.

They recruited sixty of their classmates to join the effort.

The results have been remarkable as kids from different groups in the school have come together to reach out, make new friends, and understand each other better. The "We Dine Together" initiative has garnered media attention and has now expanded to other schools.

Each of these young people are remarkable examples of what author Lewis Carroll wrote: "One of the deep secrets of life is that all really worth the doing is what we do for others."

How Can You Help Your Children Use Their Time & Talents?

1. Your example. We know a man who was struggling to figure out how to teach his children to serve others. He found a solution. Each Saturday morning he gets his three boys out of bed; loads up their truck with garden equipment, and they head out to find a widow or older person to help with yard work for two hours. He says that this single act of kindness each week has taught his sons lessons they could never learn in a textbook.

2. Consider doing family service projects regularly. To the world you may be just one person, but to one person you may be the world.

3. Make daily service an intentional part of your family culture. Ask your children to share one thing they did to serve someone that day. "Who needed you today?"

4. Point out role models who demonstrate "be a builder" behavior.

Your children can also build others with their *treasure*, or financial means. Teach your children to be charitable with their earnings, no matter how small or meager the amount.

This "treasure training" can begin at a young age, and your children will reap the benefits of this form of generosity the rest of their lives.

They'll come to embrace the concept of "If you always give, you will always have."

In one experiment with college students, researchers gave participants either a five- or twenty-dollar bill. Half the students were told to spend it by that evening on themselves, and the other half was told to spend it on others.

The group who spent the money on others "reported feeling much happier at the end of the day than those who spent the money on themselves."

In another experiment, researchers measured the rate of happiness for people who received profit-sharing bonuses of $3,000 to $8,000 from their employers. They found it was not how much money they received that predicted increased happiness but rather how the recipients spent the money.[3]

How Can You Teach Your Children to Be Charitable?

First, have them set aside a percentage of their earned allowance for charitable activities before they spend any funds on themselves.

One family we interviewed divides their children's weekly earned allowance in this manner: 25 percent to savings, 25 percent to charity, and 50 percent to spend as they like.

Decide what formula works best with your children but let them choose where they want their charity funds to go. It could go to an individual or an organization. Help them research options, and make it as real and intentional as possible.

If they want, let them save their weekly "charity money" for a longer period of time to build up more funds for a larger donation.

Help them establish a lifelong habit of giving when the amounts are small.

By doing this, your child will find it easier to give more when they have more, as they will have already created the habit of being generous. The amount they give does not matter. It's the fact that they *are* giving that really matters.

It's about their heart, not their bank account.

Consider Jon Huntsman, Sr. One of nineteen people who have donated more than $1 billion to charity, Huntsman made his wealth through the chemical products group Huntsman Corporation, which he founded in 1979.

But he didn't wait until he was rich to donate. "I have always given money away," he says. "I haven't always been wealthy—the opposite, in fact. But I have always felt that I wanted people to share it with me."

Huntsman adds, "As a young man, I was a Navy officer in Vietnam. I made $320 a month, and I always gave away $50 a month to a family I felt was in greater need than me. I've just always felt in my heart, coming from a very humble background, that there are plenty of people who need a break in life."[4]

Second, do your best to consistently model the behavior. Look for opportunities to be charitable and include your children. Help them understand the "why" behind your charitable behavior.

Third, reinforce the principle regularly. Share with your children that anonymous giving is sometimes the best way to give. Seek ways for your children to build others in such a way that the people being served never find out.

One father shared this advice with his children with respect to service: "Don't talk about it; be about it."

One teenager makes it his goal to seek ways to help others each week. His last adventure took him to McDonald's, where he went through the drive-through lane. As he reached the cashier, he asked her the cost of the meal for the person behind him.

He then gave her the money to pay for the next car's order. "Tell them to have a great day," he told the cashier. He does this on a regular basis. Can you imagine the surprise each person must feel? And you can bet this young man feels just as good or even better.[5]

Fourth, point out examples of generous behavior in others.

A sweet gesture recently lifted the morale of an entire police department. One Friday afternoon, a young boy walked into the Greenfield Police Department in Milwaukee, Wisconsin. The security camera footage shows him taking a plastic bag filled with change out of his backpack and setting it on the counter.

Assistant Police Chief Paul Schlecht told Fox6 News that the boy then said, "I want to donate my money to the police department." He left before the clerk could get his name. A Facebook post from the Greenfield Police Department identified the boy as eleven-year-old Max, who'd ridden his bike to the police station without his parents' knowledge.

Max donated the money in memory of his grandfather, an officer who had been killed in the line of duty in 1974. The donation ended up totaling $10.03 and was given to the Greenfield Police Foundation, where it will be used to help pay for training and equipment.

"We'd like to thank him for his donation and acknowledge his generosity," Schlecht told the *Milwaukee Journal Sentinel*. "It turned out to be $10.03, but it was probably all the money he had, so that's very significant."[6]

Tom Monaghan's father died when he was just four. His mother entrusted him to a Catholic orphanage because she was unable to care for him and his brother. He later graduated from high school and enrolled at the University of Michigan, but the tuition proved to be beyond his reach.

To help meet costs, he and his brother bought a pizza shop for $900. When they had expanded it to three shops, his brother sold his interest to Tom for a used Volkswagen.

Tom called his shops Domino's Pizza, and he became extremely wealthy. He bought a Bugatti car for $8.4 million, then the Detroit Tigers, a major league baseball team who won the World Series the next year.

He began construction of a massive modern home, one to rival his majestic corporate office in Ann Arbor.

Then he decided to make some changes in his life. He explained that reading the Bible and the essays of C. S. Lewis reminded him of his upbringing in the Catholic orphanage, and he wanted to devote his remaining years to service.

He sold the Tigers and the car, stopped construction on the mansion, and traded in his impressive office for a small cubicle.

He sold Domino's Pizza for more than $1 billion. Except for a small living stipend, he donated it all to Catholic Charities. He also founded a college and named it—not after himself but after Mother Mary: Ave Maria University.

Someone once asked him, "What was the most rewarding part of your amazing life? Was it winning the World Series or building Domino's Pizza or driving your Bugatti?"

His simple answer: "It wasn't the toys. I've had enough toys to know how important they aren't. *It was giving back to others*."[7]

He realized the truth of what German Holocaust victim and diarist Anne Frank wrote: "No one has ever become poor by giving."[8]

Fifth, make generosity a highlighted component of your intentional family culture.

"Our family believes it's important to share our good luck with people who are less fortunate," said one father we interviewed. You can create family-generosity traditions in your intentional family culture.

We met a mother who shared a story about her family when she was a young girl. Her parents began a family tradition of anonymously dropping off food, special treats, gifts, and even money to families during the Christmas season.

Many families like to do this around Christmastime. The peculiarity about this family was that they began this tradition when they were experiencing extreme financial hardships themselves.

The woman remembers her father telling her, "Someone else will always have less than you; find that person and share." She said that one year her family had actually been the recipient of anonymous gifts. But they still decided they could share some of what they had.

What she remembers most was the joy she and her siblings experienced as they knocked on doors and ran to ensure they were not discovered. One year, one of her siblings fell and broke his collarbone while running away from a house.

That experience is part of their "special" family memories.

You may also consider creating "charitable birthday" traditions. One family gives their children cash for their birthday with the condition that half is for them to spend on themselves, the other half to be given to a charity or needy individual of the child's choice.

They have created a family legacy and culture of being generous. This charitable family culture has now been carried on with their grandkids.

Sculpting Tool 2

Choose Kindness

Kindness can become an important tenet of your intentional family culture. Being genuinely nice to others can become a habit, a deeply felt belief, and lifelong mindset for your children.

As Mother Teresa said, "Let no one ever come to you without leaving better."

Encourage your children to look for the good in everyone they meet and for ways to be kind. "Who needs me to be kind to them today?" As your children look for the best in others, they'll find the best in themselves.

Will it always be easy for your child to have this philosophy? Is it easy for any of us? Of course not, that's part of the challenge in life, right?

We recently saw a sign at a car repair shop that read, "Some people are alive only because it's against the law to kill them!" We hope they were joking. Teach your children that everyone has value and that doing good to others is always the right thing to do.

Look for ways to model kind behavior. One mother we interviewed shared this with us:

> We taught our kids to be nice to everyone. We talked about it and we modeled it. We often reminded them, "That's what we do as a family." I can't stand cliques. I cannot stand mean girls. I will not tolerate it in my home.
>
> I think a lot of parents don't stop that, and it makes me so mad. Maybe it was because when I was growing up I had people who were unkind to me, and I swore I would never let my kids be that way because it was so painful, especially in junior high and high school.[9]

Make daily kindness a non-negotiable part of your family culture. "This is how we [insert your family name here] treat people." "This is who we [insert your family name here] are as a family."

One father we interviewed has a simple philosophy he teaches his young daughters: "At school, everyone is your friend—everybody. Okay?" One mother shared the teaching of her parents: "I was raised to treat the janitor with the same respect as the CEO."

Bullying is the polar opposite of building. No form of bullying, whether physical or emotional, personal or online, should be tolerated in your family culture.

Make it clear that [put your family name here] are builders, not bullies. Process, discuss, and role-play how to deal with any and all bullying situations.

Provide daily opportunities for your children to practice being kind. Ask your children what they did that day to show kindness to another person. Share with them one kind thing you did that day as well.

Research has shown that being kind makes children happier. One study, "Kindness is a Key to Kids' Happiness and Popularity," had some interesting conclusions:

> We all want our children to grow up to be good and happy people—hard-working, successful, and perhaps most importantly, kind to others. Now that bullying has gotten nationwide attention as a major problem for school kids, kindness seems especially important.
>
> Luckily, our study showed that encouraging kids to be kind not only makes them kinder but also makes them happier and improves their relationships with their peers.
>
> Four hundred school children, ages nine to eleven, were asked to respond to questions about how happy they were and how many of their schoolmates they would like to spend time with doing activities (a measure of peer acceptance). Then the kids were randomly divided into two groups.
>
> One group was asked to perform three acts of kindness per week, while the other was just asked to visit three places that made them happy.
>
> The children in the first group performed small acts like, "gave my Mom a hug when she was stressed by her job," or "gave someone some of my lunch," or "vacuumed the floor."
>
> After four weeks the researchers asked the children the same questions they had when the study began. For both groups, levels of well-being improved. But the kids who performed acts of kindness were also more popular.
>
> After the kindness "intervention," they were significantly more likely to be chosen by their peers as compared

to before the kindness training. In fact, the increase in their odds of being picked was equivalent to "gaining an average of 1.5 friends."

Being kind to others ended up benefiting the givers—improving their own sense of well-being, and popularity amongst their peers.[10]

Children can also learn to be kind to themselves. This might be the most important type of kindness they can share and is critically important to their lifelong emotional health and wellbeing.

Let us share one way we are intentionally teaching this concept to our grandkids. Each year at our family reunion, we introduce a new family theme for the coming year that we talk about, reinforce, and highlight during the reunion week.

At our 2019 reunion, our new theme focused on kindness, so we shared three ways they could be kind: 1) be kind to others, 2) let others be kind to you, and 3) be kind to yourself.

Anytime one of our grandkids did any of the three, we called it a "heart moment," and we celebrated it loudly and proudly. We also gave each of them a special reunion T-shirt with a big red heart on the front to reinforce the message.

Since then, whenever we spend time with them, we ask if they've had any heart moments they would like to share with us. It has been amazing to see them internalize heart moments. We get the most excited when they have been kind to themselves. We are constantly encouraging them to find more of these types of heart moments.

SCULPTING TOOL 3

Create Value

What do we mean by create value? It means your children do their best to find ways to add value to the lives of others. They find ways to become contributors and change agents and find real meaning in their lives as they create value for others.

One way for your children to become who they are capable of becoming is to help others become who they are capable of becoming.

To create value, your children can learn to develop empathy for others, to really care about other people and their feelings. The more empathy they have for others, the less critical and judgmental they will be of them, as well as themselves.

To develop empathy for others, they need to first understand their own emotions and feelings. Help your children to understand their own emotions and develop a sense of what it really means to be sad, mad, or scared. Teach them it's normal to feel that way.

As your children get older, instead of saying things like "Isn't this fun?" or "Aren't you excited about this?" help them identify *their* feelings. What if they're not excited or not having fun? You can express how you feel and then ask them how they feel, but do not tell them how to feel.

Help them understand that feelings are temporary, fleeting things. They are states, not traits. They are like the weather. Rain is real, but we know that the sun will eventually reappear. Feelings are like clouds—they will come and they will go.

You can help your children understand other people's emotions, and also model empathy and compassion for others.

Ask your children questions about how they would feel if they were in this or that situation and what would they want to happen. "Why do you think that baby is crying?" "How do you think Melinda is feeling now that her friend has moved away?"

"That woman wasn't nice to us, was she? Do you think something might have happened to her that made her feel sad today?"

To create value, your children can learn how to build relationships.

Share with your children that relationships will always be more important than things or money. As their relationships with others have the ability to become their greatest source of happiness in life, they need to invest in those relationships regularly to create strong bonds.

Strong relationships create true wealth because they make for a rich existence.

As someone once said, "The real measure of your wealth is how much you would be worth if you lost all of your money."

Social skills—the "social IQ"—are crucial to your children as they navigate their way through life. Developing social skills begins with simply being friendly or learning to have a "real" conversation with someone.

Teach your children the value of a simple smile. Smiling is a bonding agent. It builds bridges to the people around us. Smiling and laughing are contagious. A smile shows that you like yourself and are happy with the people you're interacting with.

There are also mental-health benefits. A genuine smile and laugh increase the production of serotonin, the happy hormone, and dopamine—feel good endorphins that slow cortisol production and diminish feelings of stress, anxiety, and depression.[11]

Encourage your children to smile and laugh often and to make it a goal to get others to smile and laugh as well. Ask them often, "Who did you get to smile and laugh today?" and "How did you do it?"

"Mommy, don't call me 'sweetheart'
or 'love' while the guys are here.
Just call me 'Big Bill,' okay?"

There is some interesting research on the importance of social skills for children. Researchers from Pennsylvania State and Duke Universities tracked more than seven hundred children from across the United States between kindergarten and age twenty-five.

They found a significant correlation between their social skills as kindergartners and their success as adults two decades later.

The twenty-year study showed that children who cooperated with their peers without prompting and who were helpful to others, understood their feelings, and resolved problems on their own were far more likely to earn a college degree and have a full-time job by age twenty-five than those with limited social skills.

Those with limited social skills also had a higher chance of getting arrested, binge drinking, and applying for public housing.[12]

To create value, true friends help others see the good in themselves.

Encourage your children to become a "cheerleader" for their friends and to celebrate their friends' successes. When they hear good news from a friend, children who create value genuinely think and say "Good for you."

They can learn to love instead of judge.

Teach your children that "the moment you pass a judgment on someone, it doesn't define them, it defines you." At the end of each day, have your children ask themselves, "Who did I create value for today?"

A candle loses nothing by lighting another candle.

Create an abundance mentality in your home, and help your children understand the difference between an abundance mentality and a scarcity mentality. The idea behind an abundance mentality is that there is plenty to go around for everyone, and someone else succeeding doesn't take anything away from you.

As motivational icon Zig Ziglar once said, "If you go out looking for friends, you are going to find out they are very scarce. If you go out to be a friend, you'll find them everywhere."[13]

Young people need friends. During adolescence, kids form a sense of identity based on the social networks they share with their peers as they distance themselves from their parents. A sense of belonging is right up there with food in terms of their basic needs.

To create value, your children can also learn to be aware of and notice others.

Nobody is a nobody and everybody is a somebody.

Teach your children to notice when others may need a lift in some way.

This can be as simple as a smile and hello or inviting a new or lonely person to sit at their table in the lunchroom at school.

Consider the following story:

> This year I started attending a new public high school. In one of my PE classes during the first month of school I began to notice the "outsiders." As part of the class, we had to warm up by running five or six laps around the school track.
>
> For most of the kids in the class, including me, this was no problem. But not everyone was in the greatest shape after a long summer.
>
> After finishing my laps, I was standing around and saw a girl who was behind everyone else. She struggled to keep up.

At first I didn't give her a second thought, but as I saw how much she was hurting.

I felt something in my heart. Something was telling me, *Hannah, go run with her.*

I felt really, really weird. I argued with myself, *I've never even spoken to that girl! I don't even know her name!* But I knew I had to do it, even though everyone in the class might think I was dumb.

I jogged out to the girl. She was crying and struggling to breathe, but her face radiated with surprise and thankfulness as I came up beside her. Even though I didn't know her, we finished those laps strong.[14]

Creating value includes standing up for those who cannot stand up for themselves.

Chy Johnson was a girl who was being bullied at a high school in Arizona. She was mistreated, shoved, and taunted as she walked to class; some students even threw garbage at her. Chy's mind worked at only a third-grade level because of a genetic birth defect, but she knew enough to feel hate.

Chy's mother asked teachers at the school to help stop the bullying, but it continued. She then contacted Carson Jones, the quarterback of the football team, and asked him to find out who was doing the bullying.

He said he would be happy to help, but he decided to do more. Carson and his teammates invited Chy to sit with them during lunch. Running back Tucker Workman made sure somebody walked with Chy between classes. In class, cornerback Colton Moore made sure she sat in the row right behind the team.

They brought her into their circle of friends and no one bullied Chy anymore.

And the best thing was the football players didn't tell anybody what they were doing. "I didn't know about any of this until recently," said Carson's mother. She saw an article that had been written locally. "Are you kidding me?" she said. "Why didn't you tell me this?"

As the football team went through an undefeated season and became state champions, they invited her to join them on the field after games. "I thank Carson every chance I see him," says Chy's mom. "He's an amazing young man. He's going to go far in life."[15]

These young men changed a life by their kind actions. The young woman felt valued, and her confidence soared. The team members' hearts were also softened by the experience.

They continue to be friends to this day.

What are the BENEFITS of "Be a Builder" for your children?

1. They become more unselfish.
2. They focus on building other people rather than themselves.
3. They are generous with their time, talents, and treasure.
4. They create a lifelong service mindset.
5. They are kinder to others.
6. Their hearts are softened.

TEN-SECOND SUMMARY

BE A BUILDER

1. Sharing Is Caring
2. Choose Kindness
3. Create Value

The purpose of this chapter is for this principle to eventually become a deeply rooted inner belief, Belief 7 (below), within the minds and hearts of your children.

This belief will reflect how they see, feel, and think about themselves and become part of their core identity. In other words, this is who **I AM.**

BELIEF 7

"I AM a builder of other people."

OUR INVITATION

We invite you to take a moment and consider the power and value that can be added to your children's lives as they embrace the key principle of "Be a Builder." Is there anything you could do right now to intentionally implement this principle in your family culture? Record your thoughts and ideas below:

1.

2.

3.

OUR PROMISE

When a "Be a Builder" mindset takes hold in your intentional family culture, it will create an unselfish layer of core identity within your children.

Their lives look and feel different. Their hearts are forever softened, and they will touch innumerable lives.

We make a living by what we get; we make a life by what we give.

You are Michelangelo and CAN empower your children to sculpt their lives into masterpieces!

It's now time to "put more meat on the bones" of your intentional family culture.

Shall we get to work? Let's go!

POLISHING YOUR FAMILY CULTURE OF EMPOWERMENT

"Great leaders are like great conductors—they reach beyond the notes to reach the magic in the players."
Blaine Lee

HOW CAN YOU FURTHER POLISH your intentional family culture so that your children are empowered to develop the Masterpiece Mindset and sculpt their lives into masterpieces?

How can you create "fertile soil" in your home so that the seven key principles grow into the seven deeply rooted beliefs within the minds and hearts of your children?

What's really in the "secret sauce?"

That's what this chapter is all about.

We had an interesting conversation about family culture with a father in which he asked an excellent question: "I get it—my family culture is important, and I see from your research and experience what it can look like. What I want to know is *how do I do it?*"

He had every right to know not only what makes a family culture great but also the steps needed to get there. His real question could have been "How do regular parents build amazing family cultures where their children buy enthusiastically into key family principles and vision?"

Let us consider some ways your family culture can "ignite the fire" within your children. As you digest this chapter, think about how you can introduce and incorporate the following six sculpting tools into your intentional family culture:

1. Unconditional Love
2. A Positive Environment
3. Real Engagement
4. Rules and Boundaries

5. Family Meetings
6. Spending of Family Funds

SCULPTING TOOL 1

Unconditional Love

The deepest craving of human nature is the need to be appreciated and valued. The single most important factor in helping a child develop into a vibrant adult is for them to feel loved, valued, and accepted by the key people in their lives.

Unconditional love means caring for your child without qualification. Your children should not need to earn your affection. We love our children no matter what they do or how they act. At the same time, we correct and teach them with love and patience.

On August 27, 1498, Michelangelo was commissioned by the Cardinal of Saint Denis to sculpt the *Pieta*. He was twenty-three years of age. Words cannot describe the beauty of the art piece as it must be seen in person to be truly appreciated. It is truly a masterpiece.

He wanted all those who viewed the finished sculpture to feel the unconditional love Mary had for her son, how insupportably heavy her son's dead body felt on her lap, and more importantly, the heaviness of the burden on her heart.

Upon completion nearly two years later, the white marble, polished and gleaming, illuminated his dingy room like a stain-glassed chapel. The artist had indeed created a work of beauty, later described as "the most beautiful work in marble to be seen in Rome."[1]

A young mother shares her parenting philosophy:

> From down the hallway, I could see only his feet, but I could tell my husband was kneeling down and I heard him say to our kids: "Do you know how much we love you? We love you more than anything. We love you no matter what.
>
> If someone isn't nice to you at school, or if you make a poor choice, we will always love you." I imagine he gave each of them a quick hug, and then he was off to work, closing the front door quietly behind him.
>
> When the kids make up a game at recess and won't tell our son the rules, we want him to know that we'll always tell him how to play. When our daughter doesn't get asked to a dance, we want her to know that she can always dance with us in the kitchen.
>
> We'll make up dorky handshakes and wear retro family t-shirts to show our children that we will hold their place at the family dinner table—forever.
>
> We'll do everything we can to make sure our family identity and love seeps into every corner of their souls, so they know without a doubt that they always have a place where they belong.[2]

Brené Brown, renowned writer and research professor at the University of Houston, found this in her studies:

Let me tell you what we think about children. They're hardwired for struggle when they get here. And when you hold those perfect little babies in your hand, our job is *not* to say, "Look at her, she's perfect.

My job is just to keep her perfect—make sure she makes the tennis team by fifth grade and is accepted to Yale by the seventh grade." That's not our job.

Our job is to look and say, "You know what? You're imperfect and you're wired for struggle, but you are worthy of love and belonging."

That's our job. Show me a generation of kids raised like that, and we'll end the problems I think that we see today.[3]

Please be careful not to compare your kids with other kids.

Children come with their own unique talents, gifts, and challenges and learn and progress at different rates. Some kids take off like rockets, and others linger in the middle of the bell curve.

The majority of prodigies flame out, and the majority of successful people come from the anonymous ranks of average Joes and Marys.

Comparison is the thief of joy.

Be careful about comparing your kids with each other. Each will have her or his own journey through life. Treat them as the individuals they are.

Effective parenting is doing your absolute best given your particular circumstances. Control what you can control.

Commit to the process.

It's about children progressing toward the adults they can become. The goal is always progress—not perfection.

One family had a different way of looking at the word *unconditional*:

> Mark was an exceptional math student, and as he finished junior high he was excited about going to Stuyvesant High School, a special high school in New York with a strong math and science curriculum.
>
> There, he would study math with the best teachers and talk math with the most advanced students in the city. Stuyvesant also had a program that would let him take college math courses at nearby Columbia University as soon as he was ready.
>
> But at the last moment, his parents would not let him go. They had heard that it was hard to get into Harvard University from Stuyvesant. So they made him go to a different high school.
>
> It didn't matter that he wouldn't be able to pursue his interests or develop his other talents. Only one thing mattered, and it starts with an H. In other words, "We love you, on our terms."[4]

This "conditional love" approach can be dangerous, as research confirms. G. E. Kawika Allen, assistant professor of counseling psychology, and Kenneth T. Wang, Fuller Theological Seminary psychology professor, study perfectionism in individuals and families. Here are some of their findings:

> Children who struggle to achieve family standards or don't buy into them often worry that they will compromise the family image, which can lead to anxiety and depression. Create an environment where children feel accepted and loved, whatever their level of conformity to family standards.

Be careful of too rigid achievement expectations for your children, where a message is subtly conveyed that children who don't meet the high family standard are somewhat lesser or not a full member of the family.

Every child is different and should be treated accordingly.

Unless parents communicate that it's okay to sometimes fall short of the family standard and make mistakes, they could be setting up their children for serious emotional problems in the future.

Please never forget that you are not raising robots!

Love your children unconditionally, whether they meet high family standards or not.

While parents can and should set standards and expectation levels for their family, they can also build into their family culture both *acceptance and validation* for those who struggle with, or decide they are not interested in that goal.

For a child who goes in this direction, you have to come back with more love. "We will love you always, no matter what." You can still express disappointment, but double up on love and acceptance.[5]

In other words, create a family culture that is intentional but still allows for flexibility.

Do your best to help each of your children feel connected to your family, otherwise they can feel lonely or separated. As biologist E. O. Wilson said, "People must belong to a tribe." Just like a bee goes haywire if it loses track of its hive, a human can go sideways if she loses her connection to her group.

People need people.

Yet another way to show children unconditional love is to listen with empathy whenever they want to talk. Listening attentively is a sign of respect, validation, and is empowering to those being heard.

Listening to a child helps you discover what is written upon their soul. It creates trust in the relationship.

When one of our sons was a senior in high school, we could tell he was feeling a great deal of pressure. One night he came home past curfew, and we were up waiting for him. Rather than giving him a hard time for coming home late, we opened our hearts as we could sense that he wanted to talk.

He did.

We listened as he expressed his fears and current struggles. He was the starting point guard and a captain on his school's basketball team, and the team was not performing well.

He felt personally responsible for their losing record. He was trying to get his college applications finished and had important essays to write. He had a full plate and struggled to hold it in.

Tears formed in his eyes as his frustrations came flowing out.

We shed tears as well. We felt blessed to be there for him when he needed to be listened to and validated, and it turned out to be a special bonding time for the three of us.

Listen with sensitivity as your children express their feelings. Validate their feelings and take them seriously, even though the situation may not seem serious to you. The situation and the feelings associated with it are very important to your children.

Validate, validate, validate!

Always validate their feelings first, then—and only then—address the issue or situation.

Listen first, fix later.

Dave and I were reminded of how important this principle was with two of our young granddaughters. While their mother was driving the oldest to preschool, their car was T-boned by another car whose driver had run a red light.

Fortunately, no one was seriously injured, but everybody was extremely rattled.

The car was totaled. It was a traumatic experience for these two young girls, ages four and two. Because it happened not far from our home, we were the first family members on the scene. Our son was at work and arrived shortly thereafter.

When we got there, our daughter-in-law was talking with a police officer and the girls were sitting alone in the car. After making sure everyone was okay, we gave the girls big hugs.

I then validated their feelings.

They both said it was scary and got a little teary-eyed.

After we hugged the girls again and once more validated their very real fears, I asked them, "Can you tell us what happened?" Each took a turn describing the experience from her point of view. I again asked them if they were okay, so that they could associate a positive ending with a frightening experience.

By each of them processing and describing what had happened, much of the anxiety and potential emotional trauma was diffused. Throughout the rest of the day, we had them walk through the experience with us as often as needed.

Each telling of the story became easier and more "normal" for them.

Cultural historian and literary theologian Catherine M. Wallace wrote, "Listen earnestly to anything your children want to tell you, no matter what. If you don't listen eagerly to the little stuff when they are little, they won't tell you the big stuff when they are big because to them, all of it has always been big stuff."[6]

A relationship without trust is like a car without gas. You can stay in it as long as you want, but it won't go anywhere. When there is no trust, there is no real relationship.

Another way to build trust is by asking your children their opinion on challenging situations you are dealing with, and then really listening to their ideas.

Validate and value their opinions. In successful, thriving family cultures, it is clear that every family member's opinion matters.

Speak to your children in your normal speaking voice when they are young as this can speed up their cognitive development. Help them become comfortable in adult conversations at an early age so as to help them develop social confidence in all types of settings.

SCULPTING TOOL 2

A Positive Environment

A person who feels appreciated will always do more than expected.

This kind of home environment is conducive to "good" things happening. Create an intentional family culture full of support, confidence, and respect.

Do your best to foster a "we believe in you" type atmosphere where your kids are taught and sincerely believe there is no limit to what they can accomplish. As a six-year-old girl shared, "My mother thought I was smarter than I was, so I was."

Make your home a place where your kids want to be and where your kids' friends will want to hang out. Intentionally build fun into your culture, and your children (and their friends) will naturally want to be there.

A few years ago on Father's Day, Dave asked the members of his Sunday school class at our church, "Tell me one interesting thing about your dad." One by one, each student shared something interesting about their father.

Most talked about hobbies or special talents their fathers had. And then one young man said, "I have never, ever seen my dad get mad. I have never seen him get angry or lose his temper. I have never ever heard him yell."

Everyone else in the class (including Dave) looked at him like he was crazy. The comments that followed went something like this: "You have never seen your dad get mad, ever? That's not true in my house."

"That's right," said the young man. "Never, not once." Dave was amazed because that was not true about him either or anybody else we know. We thought about this young man and his siblings, who we knew well because they are our next-door neighbors.

We thought about what kind of kids they were becoming. They are kindhearted, cheerful, responsible, well-rounded, and confident. Could the positive environment in their family culture be a reflection of their father's demeanor?

Children learn what they live.

We know that never getting angry is unrealistic for the rest of us. In fact, anger is a normal human emotion. There is nothing inherently wrong with anger in and of itself. It is our *behavior* AFTER we get angry that is potentially problematic for us and our children.

An emotion and our behavior are two completely separate things. It is the behavior that our children witness and experience that we need to manage and control.

As investment entrepreneur Charles Schwab once said, "I have yet to find the man, however exalted his station, who did not do better work and put forth greater effort under a spirit of approval than under a spirit of criticism."[7]

"HOW COME I NEVER GET CAUGHT BEIN' GOOD?"

It is easier to build a child than it is to repair an adult, choose your words carefully.

For best results, do your best to maintain at least a five-to-one ratio of positive or encouraging comments to negative or discouraging comments toward your children. This builds confidence, fuels security, and reduces anxiety.

Apparently, the tendency to hold on to negative criticism is natural for most of us. According to Dr. Roy Baumeister and researchers at Florida State University, we remember negative emotions much more strongly and in more vivid detail.

In a research paper entitled "Bad Is Stronger Than Good," Baumeister summarizes academic studies that prove we are more likely to remember criticism than praise. Baumeister found that even happy people tend to remember negative events more than positive ones.

In fact, Baumeister and his team said that when it comes to our mind, it takes about *five positive events* to make up for one negative event.[8]

Be slow to criticize and fast to appreciate your children.

Say please and thank you to them.

Seek opportunities to sincerely compliment them.

Persistent criticism is destructive and destroys confidence. When you keep criticizing your kids, they don't stop loving you, they stop loving themselves.

When criticizing or correcting, remember to do so softly and gently. Ignore the unimportant mistakes your kids make and focus on what unites, not divides. Build them up as champions, winners, and leaders.

Words can inspire, words can destroy. Choose your words carefully.

Let the walls of your home really "speak" to them.

Do your best to keep a healthy sense of humor. You're going to need it! Parenting often feels like a bumpy road, and laughter can oftentimes be your best shock absorber.

Try to:

> **Laugh** with your kids every day.
>
> **Laugh** at your mistakes, own them, and apologize if necessary. What's most important may not be what you did, but what you do after what you did.[9]
>
> **Laugh** with your kids at all the funny things that happen in life!

We received this email from a young father:

> This is an exchange between Brinley, my dramatic four-year-old daughter, and Carter, my two-year-old son. As my wife, Camille, tells it, Brinley wanted a toy Carter had; he's so cute, and he usually gives it to her if she cries hard enough.

She knew she couldn't just take it from him because he had it first, so she was crying and carrying on, screaming, "I want that!" Carter was holding the toy behind his back. Then Camille heard him say so smoothly and calmly, "Okay, but you have to say the magic word."

Brinley hates being manipulated into things, so she said, "No." Carter said again, "If you want the toy, you have to say the magic word." At that point, Brinley got right in his face and yelled, *"Please!"*

Carter stood there as stoic as ever and, with a kind expression on his face, said, "Sorry, that is not the magic word today."

Brinley's face went a deep shade of purple, and she said, "Yes, it is! I said *please!*"

Carter shook his head and said, "The magic word today is *mooo*, like the cow." At this point Camille was hunched over laughing when she heard Brinley say, "I'm not going to say that."

Carter said, "Okay, then, you can't have the toy."

Brinley huffed, took a deep breath, and yelled, "Moooo!" Carter kindly handed her the toy and walked away.

Kids are hilarious, aren't they?

T Together
E Everyone
A Achieves
M More

Wherever there is unity, there is strength.

Create a TEAM mentality among family members. "We [insert your family name here] are an unstoppable team." "We [insert your family name here] have each other's backs." One family has adopted this family motto: "We're one heck of a family, and we kick butt!"

Teach children they can reach their individual goals by striving together to reach collective family goals. As the African proverb says, "If you want to go quickly, go alone. If you want to go far, go together."

"Know why our house is the best in the neighborhood, Mommy? Because we live in it!"

Remind your children that the family boat rises and falls upon the waves together. When one succeeds, we all succeed. When one struggles, we all struggle. We rise as a family as we lift each other.

It has been satisfying for us as parents to see our sons carry this "we are a team" mindset into their adult lives. They continue to be each other's greatest cheerleaders. They have been there for each other in both good and tough times.

When Dave and I are both gone, we have no doubt they will always have each other's backs. That sure knowledge is a huge parent payday for us.

Annabella teaching our grandkids at our 2018 family reunion.

Speaking of families working together as a team:

> A minivan pulled into the only remaining campsite. Four youngsters leaped from the vehicle and began feverishly unloading gear and setting up a tent. Two kids then rushed off with their dad to gather firewood, and two others helped their mother set up the camp stove and cooking utensils.
>
> A nearby camper marveled to the father, "That is some impressive display of teamwork." "Actually," the father replied, "I have a system. No one goes to the bathroom until camp is set up."[10]

Growing up, Michelangelo had never seen a painting or sculpture of any kind in his home. In fact, his family members were self-described enemies of art because they despised the type of men who created it.

Michelangelo's father was slow to accept his son's talent and love for art and often forcefully expressed his opinion to that effect. That being said,

Michelangelo's deep loyalty toward his father and siblings always trumped the negativity he experienced at home, and he continued to serve and support them financially and otherwise until his death.

What you focus on will grow.

Or said another way: what you feed grows, and what you starve goes. It is the law of attraction. Think of a leader or teacher who was a positive influence in your life. How did that leader influence you for good? He or she probably first saw the best in you, then helped you to see it in yourself.

Dr. Haim Ginott, author of *Between Parent and Child*, says, "The single most important rule about praise is that it should only deal with children's efforts and accomplishments, not with their character or personality." Unhelpful praise includes "You're such a good child," or "You're so talented."

These type of statements make children feel uncomfortable.[11]

Dr. Carol S. Dweck had this to say about praising your children:

> According to a survey we conducted in the mid-1990s, 85 percent of parents believed that praising children's ability or intelligence when they perform well is important for making them feel smart.
>
> But our work shows that praising a child's intelligence makes a child fragile and defensive. So too, does generic praise that suggests a stable trait, such as 'You are such a good artist.'
>
> Praise can be very valuable, however, if it is worded properly. Praise for the specific process a child used to accomplish something fosters motivation and confidence by focusing children on the actions that lead to success.
>
> Such process praise may involve commending effort, strategies, focus, persistence in the face of difficulty, and willingness to take on challenges.
>
> The following are examples of such communications: "You worked really hard at that." "How did you figure it out?" "I

love your creativity." "I love the way you tell stories." "You did a good job drawing. I like the detail you added to the people's faces."

"You really studied hard for your social studies test. You read the material over several times, outlined it, and tested yourself on it. It really worked!" "I like the way you tried a lot of different strategies on that math problem until you finally got it."

"That was a hard English assignment, but you stuck with it until you got it done." "You stayed at your desk and kept your concentration. That's great!"

Parents can also teach their children to enjoy the process of learning by expressing positive views of challenges, effort, and mistakes.

Here are some examples: "Boy, this is hard—this is fun." "Oh, sorry, that was too easy—no fun. Let's do something more challenging that you can learn from." "Let's all talk about what we struggled with today and learned from. I'll go first." "Mistakes are so interesting.

Here's a wonderful mistake. Let's see what we can learn from it."[12]

Sculpting Tool 3

Real Engagement

Try to really "be there" for your children.

Be totally present when you are with them. It's not always easy these days with our ever-present smart phones. In many cases, the smart phone has already replaced your watch, camera, calendar, and clock. Don't let it replace your family!

Participate in activities your children enjoy. The respect, trust, and love you develop when they are young will come in handy later. As author Barbara Johnson has said, "To be in your child's memories tomorrow, you have to be in their lives today."

"DOES HE HAVE ADHD?"   "NO, WE JUST HAVE
                          REGULAR TV."

Spend needed time with your children to teach, train, love, and build them up. Do your best to attend their ball games, music or dance recitals, spelling bees, or any other activities.

A little time on a consistent basis spent with your children will yield significant long-term results. There is no question about that.

Margaret Archibald shared a story about her husband, Nolan, the former corporate executive we introduced earlier in the book.

> We had five sons who played varsity sports at their high school. They were involved in hundreds and hundreds of games over the years. Nolan's office was an hour and twenty minutes from our home. He also had significant responsibilities at our church.
>
> He made it a priority to be at their games. He missed a total of four games in that entire span. My sons knew they were number one to their dad. At Nolan's seventieth birthday party, I had each of our children write a tribute to their dad and read it.

One of our sons shared an experience when he played on the lacrosse team at Harvard University. The game was being played in a horrible, torrential rainstorm, and there were only two people in the bleachers cheering for the Harvard team.

One of them was his dad. He has never forgotten it.

We'd like to share another family "war story." When one of our sons was in high school, it was time for his prom. He has always been an "out of the box" type of guy, so I wasn't surprised when he asked Dave, "Instead of getting a limo for prom, we are going to rent a U-Haul truck.

Can you be our driver for the evening?" "Sure, sounds fun," responded Dave.

We laughed and asked our son for more details. He said he and his friends were going to fix up the back of the U-Haul truck with furniture and accessories. They wanted to create a prom experience their dates would never forget.

Dave loved the girls' priceless reactions as they saw the U-Haul and were then led around the back to get in, though there were some confused and concerned looks on the faces of the girls' parents!

Dave drove them to their dinner site and then finally to the dance. Their dates loved it, and other couples at the dance wished they had thought of it. Dave was definitely "there" for our son on what turned out to be a memorable evening for all involved.

A few years ago, a couple who had raised seven children on teachers' salaries were designated as the "New Hampshire Parents of the Year." When they were asked for advice on how to raise well-adjusted, responsible kids, they responded,

"Give them time, not toys. Give them time, not money."

Spending an extra hour with your kids every day versus spending an extra hour at work will pay huge dividends in your short-term and long-term relationship. Time is far more important than money because you can never get time back.

Love could really be spelled T-I-M-E.

As one father said, "The work will always come again, but childhood will not."

Sometimes your best ability is simply your availability. Always try to make time even when you don't have the time.

SCULPTING TOOL 4

Family Boundaries and Limits

Boundaries and limits are much like the walls of a fort—created to keep your children safe. Make sure they are age appropriate. Teach your children you set boundaries because you love them.

Once they come to understand the "why," they will more readily accept the "how."

Children need to know what is expected and that there are real consequences for exceeding family boundaries. They need to learn boundaries at home so that they can handle the boundaries put on them by the outside world.

One family we interviewed has these three simple rules to help their children make good choices:

1. If it's not yours, don't take it.
2. If it's not nice, don't say it.
3. If you know it's not right, don't do it.

Please do not tolerate disrespect of any kind.

Allowing disrespect even once or twice allows it to slide into your family culture. Kids who disrespect the authority of their parents will disrespect the authority of their teachers, bosses, and others in positions of authority as they go through life.

The term *discipline* originates from the Latin word *disciplinare*, which means "to teach." Most people believe discipline means *punishment*, but that is not the case.

The focus should be on teaching and behavior modification. A "disciple" is a student, not a recipient of behavioral consequences.

As a parent, you are first and foremost a *teacher*. As a teacher, you transform the moments of conflict and mistakes made by your children into opportunities for learning, problem-solving, and skill building.

Frequent, small corrections at an early age are less painful and disruptive than large course corrections later in life.

When disciplining children, bribes and threats only work temporarily. In fact, to children, threats are an invitation to repeat a forbidden act. When children are told, "If you do it once more," they do not hear "if you." They only hear "do it once more."

So make a simple statement and offer an acceptable alternative; for example, "That is not safe. Would you like to play with your truck instead?" As you effectively redirect your children, you will have fewer fights and less stress and anxiety.

It's vital children come to clearly understand family rules and consequences. You need to create realistic expectations and be consistent. As your children get older, you can begin loosening the rope.

If you don't ever trust your children, how will they ever become trustworthy?

Find the balance that works best for your family. When you let your children help set the rules and boundaries, it will help them to stay within them.

That reminds us of a story we read:

> When our son Scott was quite young, he did not care for the family rule that his bedroom had to be tidy before he could go out to play. One morning when I again explained that we lived there together and all needed to share the work, he decided he would run away.
>
> After packing his little suitcase, he marched out the back door.

From my vantage point, I could see out the living room window and I noticed that he never came into view. Soon I heard the back door open very softly, and then a little face peeked around the corner, and he said, "I'll give you one more chance to be nice to me!"[13]

The unpleasantness of a punishment may work short-term, but it is much more effective long-term to teach your kids to own and correct their mistakes.

Instead of approaching misbehavior with "What can I do to you so you'll learn a lesson?" approach it with "How can we solve this problem?"

This teaches kids that mistakes are fixable and not to be feared.

As author L. R. Knost said, "Discipline is helping a child solve a problem. Punishment is making a child suffer for having a problem. To raise problem solvers, focus on solutions, not retribution."[14]

Your response to bad behavior creates different long-term effects for them. When children cause harm, they typically feel one of two emotions: shame or guilt.

These emotions are *not* interchangeable. Research led by George Mason University psychology professor June Price Tangney reveals that they have very different causes and consequences.

Shame is "I am a bad person." Guilt is "I have done a bad thing." Shame is a negative judgment about the core self and is devastating, as negative beliefs are created.

Shame makes children feel small and worthless, and they respond by either lashing out at the target or escaping the situation altogether.

In contrast, guilt is a negative judgment about an action, which can be repaired by engaging in better behavior. When children feel guilt, they tend to feel remorse and regret, empathize with the person they have harmed, and aim to make it right.

If we want our children to care about others, we need to teach them to feel guilt rather than shame when they misbehave. In a review of research on emotions and moral development, psychologist Nancy Eisenberg suggests that shame emerges when parents express anger, withdraw love, or try to assert power through threats of punishment.

Children may begin to believe they are bad people.[15]

The following story illustrates this principle:

> One time, three of my buddies and I egged the house of the assistant principal. We got caught. When they called us all into the principal's office, they told us to call our parents and get them to the school immediately.
>
> I remember calling my dad at work and telling him to come to the school because I was in trouble.
>
> When all the parents and kids were in the conference room, the assistant principal told the story of his house getting egged and that we were the ones to blame. One of the mothers said, "That is impossible. My son would never do that."
>
> In contrast, my dad looked at me and asked, "Did you do it?"
>
> I looked him in the eye and said, "Yes, sir, I did."
>
> The assistant principal screamed, "You have a bad kid there!"
>
> I will never forget my dad's fist exploding on the table in front of him, and him saying, "I do *not* have a bad kid here. I have a good kid who did a bad thing."[16]

The most effective response to bad behavior is to express disappointment in the action without getting angry or lashing out.

According to independent reviews by Professor Eisenberg and David R. Shaffer, parents can raise caring children by expressing disappointment, explaining why the behavior was wrong, explaining how it affected others, and helping the children figure out how they can rectify the situation.

This enables children to develop standards for judging their actions and feelings of empathy and responsibility for others. The beauty of expressing disappointment is that it communicates disapproval of the bad behavior coupled with high expectations and the potential for improvement:

"You're a good person, even if you did a bad thing, and I know you can do better."[17]

Sculpting Tool 5

Family Meetings

Try to create a family tradition where your family spends time together at least one evening a week—if possible, on the same day each week. Put it on your family calendar.

It will be challenging, but we promise you it will pay both short- and long-term dividends for your children and family.

Here are some ideas of what you can do in your family meeting. Pick and choose what might work with your family, and remember *there is no set format or time frame.*

It could be from fifteen minutes to an hour-plus, depending on the how the evening is going, or the activity that has been planned. Be flexible.

- Coordinate the family calendar for the coming week.

- Address any current family challenges or concerns. Give children time to share their issues without judgment or ridicule.

- Share a short message/teaching moment that incorporates one or more of the seven key family principles. Test your children on their knowledge of the principles by asking them to recite them. Make it a game and have fun.

- Play other fun games as well and be sure to serve treats! Rotate the assignment so that different family members have the opportunity to share the message/teaching moment on a given week.

- At least once a month on your family meeting night, go out as a family and do something fun. Or participate in a family service project in your community.

- Share stories from your life or your ancestors' lives.

- Create your own family slogans or mottos. Here are some examples:

  "We Warners are a team."
  "Sumsions never give up!"
  "Holmoes are loyal to family, faith, and friends."
  "Hagens can do hard things."
  "Popes are participators."

Have fun with them and connect them to the seven key principles. When your slogans or mottos become part of your family culture, your kids will never forget them and they will be carried on to future generations.

Consider creating a family mission statement. Your mission statement can answer the following questions: What do we stand for as a family? Who do we want to be as a family? A simple, one-sentence statement is all that is necessary.

Stephen M. R. Covey did not need to read one of his father's books to learn how to be an effective father—he learned by example: "My father was a great example of a patriarch who never stopped teaching. We carried on a lot of traditions he established, and also have created some of our own," said Stephen.

"It seems like so many people who have kids now don't think about establishing family traditions because life comes at you so fast, it's hard not to be reactive."

One of the traditions Stephen learned from his father was the importance of creating a family mission statement. He and his wife Jeri have five children, and they wanted their family to focus on their mission statement, which they have prominently displayed on pictures and signs in their home.

"To live, to love, to learn, to leave a legacy" is their straightforward family mission statement. "What that includes is the body, heart, mind, and spirit," Covey said. "That's something we established along the way that has turned out to be significant for our family."

Each week in their family meeting, they review their mission statement. One of their children is called on to stand up and recite it at the beginning of the meeting. They also recite other family mottos and slogans.[18]

In your family meetings, you can role-play decisions your children may face in the future, including peer-pressure situations, bullying confrontations, or social media interactions.

Or create a family flag with family mottos painted by your children like we did. Our boys loved creating our family flag—they were extremely creative and very messy! It became a memorable family bonding experience.

The structure of your family meeting is not as important as the time spent together.

Do your best to make it a fun and meaningful experience for all. Some nights will work better than others.

SCULPTING TOOL 6

Spending of Family Funds

When it comes to spending family resources, here is some simple advice: spend funds on experiences—not things—that teach and reinforce the right lessons.

Experiences will become more meaningful, more important, and better remembered by your children than things.

Happiness derived from childhood experiences is far more valuable than the fleeting excitement of toys under the Christmas tree. Providing experiences that involve time spent as a family rather than giving toys will create more overall happiness and joy for your children.

You will not be able to remember memories you did not create.

Vacations, reunions, and learning excursions are great examples. Don't forget to document the experiences with photo books, journals, videos, etc. It's simple and inexpensive to do these days. You will find your children look at these reminders often as a way of reliving the experiences.

One year, my youngest son and I attended the Final Four of the men's NCAA college basketball tournament in San Antonio, Texas. I decided I wanted to have great seats for once in my life, so I went to a ticket broker. We ended up in the front row, midcourt.

There were no better seats in the arena.

They were more expensive but worth every penny because of the unbelievable experience. The two national semifinal games were on Saturday night, and the championship game was on Monday night. We sat in those seats for all the games.

Just before the first game started on Saturday evening, we heard a little commotion behind us and saw a family with bodyguards walking down the stairs toward us. We didn't know who they were. They ended up having the seats right next to us.

It was Rick Perry, the governor of Texas, and his family. It was fun getting to know them and hanging out with them during the games. My son, who loves politics, was in heaven.

Governor Perry later went on to run for president of the United States, and became secretary of energy.

When the championship game was over, my son was able to "sneak" out onto the court while the winning team was celebrating their national championship and cutting down the nets. Confetti from the rafters rained down upon him.

It was a priceless bonding experience for us.

Remember, you show your kids what's most important to you by how you spend your money, so be careful—they are always watching!

There are some interesting government statistics on what it costs to raise a child these days. According to a U.S. Department of Agriculture study, a child born in 2015 will cost his parents $233,610, on average, from birth to age seventeen.

Higher-income families are expected to spend on average $372,210. These stats don't even include the annual cost of college, which the government estimates is $45,370 for a private college and $20,090 for a public college.[19]

We're not sure if we trust government statistics, but we do know that raising kids is expensive. It's probably even more costly now. Spend your hard-earned money on experiences that prepare your children for long-term success.

The most important investment you will ever make is in your family.

How much of an investment are you willing to make? What would you give to have confident, kind, resilient kids who are able to live a masterpiece of a life?

What would you be willing to give up if one of your children is struggling?

One of our good friends was asked that exact question. He has seven children who are all responsible individuals doing positive things with their lives. On the other hand, he has an extremely wealthy neighbor whose children have struggled mightily and have given their parents a lifetime of heartache.

Our friend was asked by his neighbor, "How much would you take for one of your good kids?" It was a hypothetical question and was said jokingly—sort of.

The neighbor went on to tell our friend that he and his wife would gladly give up all their wealth if their children had made different choices and taken different paths in their lives.

The father looked back and saw things that they as parents could have done differently that may have led to different results. He said he would absolutely change some of the priorities in their family culture if he could get a do-over.

But at that point, it was too late.

Always look for ways to invest in yourself and your children.

Some Final Advice

1. Focus on your children's progress, not on perfection. As was mentioned earlier, never forget that:

    There are no guarantees or warranties in parenting.
    There is no one-size-fits-all parenting model. Why?
    Because every child comes wired differently and has agency to make their own decisions.

2. You will find great empowerment in focusing on the parenting process rather than on the parenting outcome. You may recall that we

have discussed this process concept throughout the book. The process are the things you can control, the outcome the things you cannot.

Control what you can control.

Commit to the process.

Focusing on things you cannot control is frustrating and counterproductive, whereas focusing on the things you can control is confidence building and intentional.

Experience has taught us that real success (in all walks of life) comes from locking in on the process and letting the outcome take care of itself.

3. You are doing better than you think you are! Remember to maintain a long-term perspective when it comes to your parenting efforts. As French playwright Moliere wrote, "The trees that are slow to grow bear the best fruit."

    You can't microwave the maturation process. It simply takes time. Some days you will wonder if it will all work out, but it will.

"Don't worry, Mommy. I'll get you
some for Christmas."

Will you make mistakes as a parent? Why wouldn't you? Just as kids grow by making mistakes, so do parents. Welcome to the club! Own your mistakes, learn from them, and move on.

Always remember that you are a well-intentioned parent. We repeat, you are good enough! Do not beat yourself up or put yourself down.

In fact, at the end of a rough day, take a moment to sit back and reflect on three things you did well that day, then identify one thing you can improve on the next day.

And maybe go eat some chocolate!

Your goal is not to raise perfect children. Your goal is to raise children who can deal with an imperfect world.

One mother related this experience:

> One spring afternoon I was packing my car to begin shuttling my five young children to and from lessons and practices. As I loaded soccer cleats and dance bags, I noticed a mother duck and her ducklings waddling down the sidewalk of our suburban neighborhood.

As I watched, the mother duck began to cross the road. Unfortunately, she chose a gutter grate for her crosswalk, and as she passed over it, her babies followed. Four of her ducklings slipped helplessly between the bars of the grate.

When the mother reached the other side, she realized she was missing some of her little ones, and she could hear their muffled peeps. Totally oblivious of her mistake, she crossed back across the drainage grate, looking for her missing ducklings, and lost two more.

With horror and some disgust at her poor judgment, I went to the grate to see if I could lift it. Although I used all my strength, the grate barely budged, and I was late to pick up one of my kids.

Figuring I could fix the situation later when I wasn't so rushed, I hopped in the car while muttering self-righteously, "She doesn't deserve to be a mother." During the next hour and a half, I made many recurring mistakes.

When I snapped at one of my kids for teasing another, my words echoed in my ears: "She doesn't deserve to be a mother."

Suddenly I felt overwhelming compassion for that mother duck. She was trying to navigate the world with instincts she was given, just as I was. But sometimes those instincts simply weren't enough, and it was our children who suffered.

I resolved to get the grate off somehow so I could lift the ducklings out. As I rounded the corner to our street, I saw a small group gathered.

My neighbor had lifted the grate, climbed inside the drainage tunnel, and was gently lifting the ducklings to safety. The frightened little birds scrambled to find their mother, who was pacing nervously in a nearby bush.

She hadn't asked for help, but my neighbor had stepped in when her protection was simply not enough.

I was overcome with emotion as I thought of others who have done the same for my children and for me.

Sometimes we just come up short, even when we have the best intentions and try our hardest. It comforts me to know that my shortcomings will not ruin my children.[20]

4. Please do not compare yourself to other parents. We often see the best in them and the worst in ourselves. Every parent has his or her own respective parenting journey, and each parent needs to own and embrace their unique path.

    You really can become the parent you are capable of becoming. As we are prone to say, comparison really is the thief of joy!

This mother's response to a newspaper article sums it up well:

Once, when I was leaving church with several small children, a woman behind me, also with small children, sighed and said, "There goes my example of perfect motherhood." I looked around to see who she was talking about.

When I saw that it was me, I told her very firmly, "Don't do that to yourself, and don't do that to me. It is not fair to either one of us. You see what I want you to see. You do not see my unmade beds. You do not see me at home when I yell at my kids.

You do not see me get impatient, and you don't see my messy closets. You see what I want you to see, and what you see is not the complete truth." We don't have to be perfect. We need to strive to make each day a little bit better than before while realizing that we will all have our bad days too.

It's okay to be you, and it is okay to be me, and we do not need to be false in who we are. Having that attitude has really helped me deal with all my anxiety and stresses in life.[21]

You don't inspire others by being perfect. You inspire others by how you deal with your imperfections.

What Other Cultures Are You Competing With?

Society: Our current society tells us that our achievements in our career are more important than the achievements in our families. That is simply not true. You can be successful both at work and at home.

Do not give your family your "leftover" time.

Peers: Your children's peers' families may see things differently than you do. That's okay. This creates excellent "teaching" moments and opportunities for conversations with your children.

Media: The television shows, movies, video games, music, and social media your children absorb often send messages not in alignment with your key family principles and culture. Again, these provide good teaching opportunities as to the "why."

Your ex-spouse's culture: What if you are divorced and your ex sees things differently than you? Is their idea of family culture different than yours? When your child spends time with them, are they different when they come back to you?

This can be a fragile, tricky situation, but do your best to deal with it in a positive, productive manner.

Your new spouse's culture: What if you are in a blended family and he or she comes from a significantly different family culture from yours? How can these differences affect your children and your new stepchildren?

You need to work to get on the same page and create your *own* new family culture.

Which culture will win? Will it be your intentional family culture or one of the others? You have a significant influence on the outcome. Guard and protect your family culture from the creeping in of other cultures.

Protect it from drifting away from your key family principles.

The good news? You can raise children that are society, peer, and social media culture resistant!

Stay Committed!

Please never forget that your intentional family culture is not a one-and-done-type initiative. Family culture is constantly evolving and is based upon daily, weekly, and monthly experiences.

Without constant attention, it is possible for even the most diligent families to lose some of the secret sauce that made them special in the first place. An empowering family culture takes time and a focused effort to create and maintain.

You can do this.

As you begin to change your family culture, try to keep it simple. Complexity is the enemy of execution. You cannot change your entire family culture overnight. You can't microwave the process. Be patient.

Small behavior changes consistently executed over time will get your family culture where you want it to be.

TEN-SECOND SUMMARY

POLISHING YOUR FAMILY CULTURE OF EMPOWERMENT

1. Unconditional Love
2. A Positive Environment
3. Real Engagement
4. Family Rules and Boundaries
5. Family Meetings
6. Spending of Family Funds

Your family culture will trump anything else you will ever do as a parent.

Whether you are a single parent, married, or parenting with a partner, your family culture will certainly be tested. Some days it will be difficult to stay the course, but you can do it!

Hard is good, right? On those days, take a moment to reflect on your "why" for creating your intentional family culture in the first place, and keep moving forward.

If your why is powerful enough, the how becomes easier.

Consider what it can do for your children and how critical it is to your goal of raising kids who develop the Masterpiece Mindset.

And finally, remember the inspired words of Winston Churchill: "Never, never, never, give up!"

Your intentional family culture can empower your children to develop the Masterpiece Mindset and sculpt their lives into masterpieces.

Someday your kids (and grandkids) will thank you for your commitment to your intentional family culture.

Maybe one year at your summer family reunion, you, your children and your grandchildren will all be wearing T-shirts with your family name on the back, and the phrase "Created By Culture" on the front!

Your consistent, deliberate efforts at maintaining your intentional family culture will lead your children to knowing who they are, where they are going, and how to get there. That is extremely powerful.

Your children can find their potential and become their best selves and who they are capable of becoming.

And finally, as coach Pete Carroll said, "If you have an undying belief that you are going to create something unique and special in your world, you will!"

That perfectly describes your intentional family culture.

Trust the process, and we promise you'll like the outcome!

You are Michelangelo and CAN empower your children to sculpt their lives into masterpieces!

Dave and Annabella have a video message for you that relates to this chapter. Please go to themasterpiecemindset.com to view it.

YOU ARE MICHELANGELO!

*"A masterpiece does not unfurl its wings immediately.
It takes time. It will fly when it's ready."*
A. D. Posey

AFTER NEARLY TWO YEARS OF dedicated work, Michelangelo's *Pieta* was finally finished. Crowds gathered from long distances to see the masterpiece displayed at St. Peter's in Rome.

One afternoon Michelangelo wandered into the church and saw a family with several grown children standing in front of his *Pieta*, making elaborate gestures with their hands. He went to their side to eavesdrop. "But who made it?" asked one of the children.

"I tell you I recognize the work," said the mother of the family. "It is by that fellow from Osteno, who makes all the tombstones."

Her husband waved the fingers of both his hands loosely, shaking off this idea as a dog shakes off water. "No, no, it is one of our country-men, Cristoforo Solari, called 'The Hunchback,' from Milan. He has done many of them."

That same evening, Michelangelo went back to the church. Hiding behind a column, he waited for the closing hour when he would be locked in for the night. He had brought with him a candle and his hammer and chisel.

And the whole night through, he diligently carved his name on the band lying across the Virgin's breast:

Michael Angelus Bonarotus Florentinus Faciebat.

On the very heart of the Madonna, where all could see it, he carved in clear letters: "Michelangelo Buonarroti of Florence made this." It was the first and last time he would ever mark one of his sculptures with his name.

No one would ever wonder again who had created the masterpiece.[1]

Like Michelangelo, you have the privilege of putting your "personal stamp" on each of your children by creating an intentional family culture within your home that empowers them to sculpt their lives into masterpieces.

You have the unique opportunity to light the fire within their minds and hearts that will lead them to develop the Masterpiece Mindset.

What can the Masterpiece Mindset do for your children?

With the Masterpiece Mindset, your children develop a vision of their possibilities and approach life without fearing what lies ahead.

They are not afraid to fail, and they look forward to the challenge of doing hard things. They bring their best effort to everything they do and are extremely resilient in the face of disappointment.

They develop true empathy and compassion for others. They are kind, teachable, humble, and grateful for what they have. They look for ways to bring out the best in other people and create value for them.

They don't limit themselves or let the opinions of others affect them. They become self-motivated, disciplined, and responsible. They are finishers.

They develop deep confidence in themselves and experience less anxiety and stress as they embrace the natural ebb and flow of life. They relish the beauty of unselfish service, develop a passion for life that's contagious, and experience lives of purpose and value.

These children are dreamers and doers. They become assertive leaders who live their lives with no regrets about what-ifs, and come to find out who they really are and who and what they can become.

They become fearless to the point that life is truly a grand adventure for them.

Is this really possible for your children?

It is—with your visionary leadership, intentional commitment, and principle-based parenting. Your children can become who they are capable of becoming, *whatever that looks like for them individually.*

Everything in your children's lives begins and ends with what is inside their minds. Their lives are a result of the stories they tell themselves, about themselves, every single day.

At the end of the day, the quality and trajectory of your children's lives will come down to their *mindset*—how they see, think, and feel about themselves.

Their core identity. ("This is who I AM…")

With the Masterpiece Mindset, your children can create for themselves a life that's a masterpiece. As a parent, does it get any better than that?

Let's review the **VIP PLAN**, which acts as your overarching parent roadmap:

V Vision

I Intentional Family Culture

P Principles

VISION

It was July 4, 1952. Florence Chadwick, who had previously swum the English Channel, was now attempting the twenty-one-mile swim from the Southern California coast to Catalina Island. The water was a frigid forty-eight degrees, the fog thick, visibility almost nil.

Just a half mile from her destination, she became discouraged and quit.

The next day, reporters clamored around her, asking why she had given up. Had it been the cold water or the distance? It was neither. Instead, she responded, "I was licked by the fog." She then talked about a similar experience while swimming the English Channel, when the fog had likewise engulfed her.

She was exhausted.

As she was about to reach for her father's hand in the nearby boat, he pointed to the shore, and she raised her head out of the water just long enough to see the land ahead. With that new clear vision, she pressed on and became the first woman to conquer the Channel.[2]

Like Florence Chadwick, you can develop a clear vision of your children's potential. This vision for your children becomes your *"why"* for doing what you do as a parent every single day. If your why is powerful enough, the how becomes easier.

What is your **HOW?** How can you empower your children to sculpt their lives into masterpieces? The answer lies below.

INTENTIONAL FAMILY CULTURE

You can, in essence, "re-model" your home and the future lives of your children by building an empowering intentional family culture.

Be intentional about being intentional.

Your intentional family culture is the potential masterpiece that you as a parent can sculpt. It is your equivalent of Michelangelo's David. *You sculpt an environment in your home that empowers your children to sculpt their lives into masterpieces.*

Here is a story of how a single mother changed the future trajectory of her family by implementing one intentional change into their family culture.

One of her sons, Ben, said of himself, "I was the worst student in my whole fifth-grade class." One day he took a math test consisting of thirty problems. The student behind him corrected it and handed it back to Ben.

The teacher, Mrs. Williamson, called each student's name; each was to report his or her own score. Finally, she got to Ben. Out of embarrassment, he mumbled the answer. Mrs. Williamson, thinking he had said "nine," replied that for Ben to score nine out of thirty was a wonderful improvement.

The student behind Ben then yelled out, "Not nine! He got *none* right." Ben wanted to drop through the floor.

At the same time, Ben's mother, Sonya, faced obstacles of her own. One of twenty-four children in her family, she had only a third-grade education and could not read.

She had married at the young age of thirteen, was now divorced, and had two sons she was raising in the ghettos of Detroit. Nonetheless, she was fiercely self-reliant and had a firm belief that God would help her and her sons if they did their part.

One day, a turning point came in Sonya's life and that of her sons. It dawned on her that the successful people for whom she cleaned homes had libraries—they read.

After work that day, she went home and turned off the television Ben and his brother were watching and said, "You boys are watching too much television.

From now on you can watch three programs a week. In your free time you will go to the library. You will read two books a week and give me a report."

Shocked, the boys protested, complained, and argued, but to no avail. Ben had never read a book in his entire life except when required to do so at school. He reflects, "She laid down the law. I didn't like it, but her determination to see us improve changed the course of my life."

And what a change it made. By the seventh grade, Ben was at the top of his class. He went on to attend Yale University on a scholarship and Johns Hopkins Medical School, where at age thirty-three he became chief of pediatric neurosurgery and a world-renowned surgeon.

In fact, Ben Carson was the first surgeon to separate twins joined at the head. In 2008 he was given the Presidential Medal of Freedom by President George W. Bush. In 2016, he ran for president of the United States, and was later named the Secretary of Housing and Urban Development.

How was all this possible? "Between the covers of those books," he said, "*I could go anywhere, I could be anybody, I could do anything.*"[3]

This mother "intentionally" made reading, learning, and education a component of their family culture—a simple change that led to dramatic results for her sons.

Their mindset changed, and they developed a new vision of their possibilities. They came to deeply believe that they could do anything and be anybody in spite of their challenging circumstances.

Your family culture will trump anything else you ever do as a parent.

Building an intentional family culture in your home leads us to the final part of our parenting plan, which is your **WHAT.**

What specifically do you teach your children that will lead them to develop the Masterpiece Mindset and become who they are capable of becoming? The answer lies below.

PRINCIPLES

You intentionally teach seven key principles to your children.

These seven key principles are powerful, practical, and timeless and become the foundation of your intentional family culture.

Below is a story of how key family principles taught at home played out in a real-life decision of a young man.

When this young man was fourteen, he was chosen to play on an all-star basketball team. The summer after he finished eighth grade, the team competed in tournaments throughout the United States. One tournament was held at Duke University in Durham, North Carolina.

One evening, one of the players invited all of his teammates to his hotel room to watch a movie. When the young man saw that it was pornographic, he got up and left the room, and one of his teammates followed him.

When the young man returned home from the trip, his parents asked how the tournament had gone both for him personally and for his team. He responded, "Good, we played well." Later that evening, the phone rang at their home.

Yes, in those days phones were on the wall!

It was the father of the teammate who had followed the young man out of the hotel room where the movie was being shown. He related the experience and thanked the father for the way he had raised his son.

He shared that his son admitted he would not have left the hotel room had his son not led the way.

The father was surprised, as his son had not even mentioned the experience. After hanging up the phone, he shared the conversation with his wife, and they went and asked their son about it. Their son confirmed, "Yes, that is exactly what happened."

They asked why he'd left the hotel room. They pointed out that they, as his parents, would have never known if he had stayed and watched the movie.

His response was, "There are things you taught me and things I want to do in my life, and I knew that if I stayed and watched that movie, it might lead me down a path I did not want to go."

They congratulated their son on his wise, mature choice. How many fourteen-year-old boys do you know who would have made that same decision?

One of the benefits of the Masterpiece Mindset is that children become comfortable in their own skin as well as assertive and confident leaders. They first learn to lead themselves, and then lead others.

This young man clearly knew who he was (this is who **I AM**), and had a vision of his future possibilities. His inner beliefs about himself and his core identity had already begun to form.

A life-changing mindset was in the process of being built.

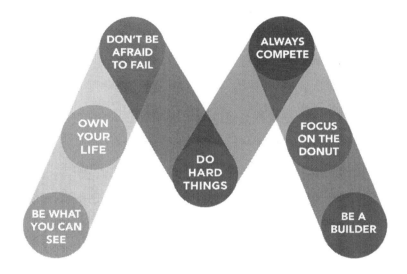

You will witness tremendous change as the seven key principles are introduced and implemented in the lives of your children. They can become deeply entrenched anchors they secure themselves by.

When your children leave your home, they will flourish without you because the seven key principles they have learned and lived in your intentional family culture will become deeply imbedded within their minds and hearts.

Whatever you repeat, you reinforce.

Recognize, highlight, and celebrate each time your children's behavior is in alignment with the seven key principles. Make regular use of the "sculpting tools" in your parenting "tool bag" to introduce, teach, and reinforce the seven key principles.

As these principles in effect, "seep into your children's bones," seven deeply rooted beliefs are formed, and a **powerful core identity** is built.

The Masterpiece Mindset is a combination of these seven beliefs.

When your children come to understand who they really are, it is much easier for them to see who they can eventually become.

Children who know who they are and have a vision for what they can become are built, not born. Be patient and **focus on their progress, not on perfection,** and on who they can eventually "become."

The goal with the seven key principles is that they eventually become these seven deeply rooted beliefs within your children's minds:

BELIEF 1
I AM a person who can be what I can see in my mind.

BELIEF 2
I AM the owner of my life.

BELIEF 3
I AM not afraid to fail.

BELIEF 4
I AM a person who can do hard things.

BELIEF 5
I AM a person who competes in everything I do.

BELIEF 6
I AM grateful for who I am and what I have.

BELIEF 7
I AM a builder of other people.

That is the Masterpiece Mindset!

Within your intentional family culture, let's take one last look at your children's pathway to the Masterpiece Mindset:

7 Principles > Experiences > 7 Beliefs > The Masterpiece Mindset

Seven key principles taught to your children.
Experiences that affirm and reinforce the seven key principles.
Seven beliefs resulting from the "right" kind of experiences.
The Masterpiece Mindset is the end result.

A masterpiece of a life is then possible for your children.

Your children come to know who they really are, where they are going, and how they are going to get there.

They become the best version of themselves.

They become who they are capable of becoming.

With this core identity, watch out, world! It will be fun for you as a parent to stand back and watch what happens as their lives unfold in front of you. Nice work, Mom and/or Dad!

THE MASTERPIECE MINDSET gives your children the ability to truly sculpt their lives into masterpieces, *whatever that looks like for them individually.*

They will find out the answers to these questions:

"Who were YOU born to be"
"What were YOU born to do?"
"Who are YOU capable of becoming?"

The greatest inheritance you can ever give your children is the Masterpiece Mindset. You are empowering them to bring out the very best in themselves. You are creating a family legacy that will transform future generations of your family.

So what do you think?
Can you do this?
You absolutely can!

Whether you are a single parent, married, or parenting with a partner, trust this parenting process. You will love the results.

Always try to **control what you can control.**
Commit to the process.

Never forget that you will *always* be a **VIP** in the eyes of your children.

Bring out the best in yourself as a parent so your children can be empowered to bring out the best in themselves. You *can* become the parent you are capable of becoming.

You can live your own life with vision, intention and the seven key principles.

It is better for your children to see a sermon rather than hear a sermon.

And finally, a father we interviewed, Neal Warner, asked us to share his story:

> Some are fortunate to miss a call from death. I know the exact date and time that death called me.
>
> It was on a Thursday night at 2:43 a.m. when I abruptly woke up with intense pain in my chest.
>
> I could not move or speak. It felt like the type of muscle cramp I would get in my leg, but the epicenter of the pain was on the left side of my chest.
>
> At first I thought it was just indigestion, so I tried to ride it out, but the tightness only intensified.
>
> I got out of bed and tried to walk but only managed to take two steps before I bent over and put hands on my knees. I repeatedly called out my wife's name until she woke up.
>
> My wife, Jeannie, said to me, "What is going on? Are you okay? Do I need to call an ambulance?"
>
> I was light-headed and disoriented. All I could say were the words "Please help me. Help me, please. I think I'm having a heart attack."
>
> She scrambled to find her phone and called 911.
>
> A clear thought came to me. "Am I really dying?" In that split second, I realized that nothing else in life mattered to me but my wife and three children.

"If I never see my children again, what will I have left them? As a father, had I done everything I could to teach them what they needed to lead productive and happy lives?"

I had the consuming thought that I had not done enough. In my mind, I shouted, "I need more time. I need more time with my children!"

I cannot say with certainty how close I came to dying, but I can tell you the overwhelming feeling I had was that I had not made my children enough of a priority in my life.

That needed to change, and the time to change was RIGHT NOW!

And it did.

Your children and grandchildren will be forever grateful for your decision to start **TODAY** to internalize, implement, and live by the VIP plan and the overarching principles shared in this book.

We can't tell you how excited we are for you and your children. Even though we have never met you personally, we want you to know we believe in you.

Thank you for investing your time with us. That shows a great commitment to your children, and they are lucky to have you as their VIP parent.

Nice job Michelangelo!

We wish you the very best in your parenting quest.

You are Michelangelo and CAN empower your children to sculpt their lives into Masterpieces!

What's the next step for you?

Are you ready to take your kids and family to the next level?

Are you ready to bring out the best in yourself as a parent so you can empower your children to bring out the best in themselves?

Are you ready to create a home environment that will help your children have less anxiety, depression or suicidal thoughts?

Are you ready to build an empowering *intentional* family culture that will transform your family for generations?

We can teach you how.

**Come join us right now at
themasterpiecemindset.com to find out
how these things are possible for you!**

Acknowledgments

Many hands, minds, and hearts have contributed to getting this book across the finish line; thank you to each one of you, named and unnamed!

To our team of professional editors: Shelly Davis, Chersti Nieveen, and Neil Warner. Each of you added great insight and value along the way. Thank you!

To Angela and the five-star EE team—Michele, Kathy, and Michelle—your professional expertise was invaluable! To Jed Morley for his creative thoughts and inspired ideas—we wouldn't be here without you! To John Kung, thank you for your patience with the graphic designs and formatting! To Josh Carr for his marketing genius!

To the many friends who regularly and gently asked us, "When is the book going to be done?" Thanks for your encouragement and for pushing us!

And high fives to the many mothers and/or fathers who graciously gave of their time to be interviewed. Your significant contributions to the book are deeply appreciated.

And finally to Seth Ellsworth, the young father whose lunch meeting and questions inspired the vision for this book. Thanks, brother!

Notes

Catching a Glimpse of Your Potential Masterpiece

Epigraph: BraveHeart, directed by Mel Gibson (1995, California: Paramount Pictures, 2000), DVD.

1. David B. Haight, "Your Purpose and Responsibility" (Brigham Young University fireside, September 4, 1977), 2–3.

The VIP Plan

Epigraph: "Mastering the Pieces of Public Speaking," accessed April 11, 2019, https://craigvalentine.com/mastering-the-pieces-of-public-speaking/.

1. Stephen Palmer, "Would you pass the 'Red Shirt Warrior' test?" Life Manifestos, September 9, 2013, 2–3.

Building Your "Intentional" Family Culture

Epigraph: S. Chris Edmonds, *The Culture Engine* (Hoboken, NJ: John Wiley and Sons, 2014).

1. Theodore Roosevelt in a letter to his friend William Sturgis Bigelow on March 29, 1898.

2. Carol S. Dweck, *Mindset* (New York: Random House, 2006), 3.

3. Phone interview with Nolan & Margaret Archibald, February 17, 2015.

4. Steve Densley, "The Integrity of a Dog's Tail," *Daily Herald*, June 9, 2013, E2.

5. Sonia Sotomayer, *My Beloved World* (New York: Knopf/Borzoi, 2013), 178.

6. Sotomayer, *My Beloved World.*

7. Bob Rotella, *How Champions Think* (New York: Simon & Shuster, 2015), 15.

8. Craig Manning, "The Fearless Mind," August 27, 2014; blog post.

9. David B. Williams, "Michelangelo's Marble Madness—Part 2," December 7, 2011, GeologyWriter.com.

Principle 1

1. Bob Rotella, *How Champions Think* (New York: Simon & Shuster, 2015), 15.

2. Pete Carroll, *Win Forever* (New York: Portfolio/Penguin 2011), 185.

3. Covey, Stephen M. R. and Jeri, personal interview on September 4, 2015.

4. Carli Lloyd, *When Nobody Was Watching* (Boston New York: Houghton Mifflin Harcourt 2016), 83-84

5. Harvey Mackay, "Realize your Max Potential," *Daily Herald*, October 24, 2018

6. Interview with Alexa von Tobel, conducted and condensed by Adam Bryant in 2015. A version of this article appeared in print on April 19, 2015 in the *New York Times*.

7. John Goddard, *The Survivor: 21 Spine Chilling Adventures on the Edge of Death,* (Deerfield Beach, FL: Health Connections, Inc. 2001).

8. Stephen Palmer, "When All Else Fails," *Life Manifestos,* August 19, 2013.

9. Tom Verducci, "Chosen One," *Sports Illustrated,* June 8, 2009.

10. Marianne Williamson, *A Return to Love: Reflections on the Principles of a Course of Miracles* (New York: Harper Collins 1992), 190–91.

11. Rotella, *How Champions Think*, 113.

Principle 2

1. Scott Peterson, personal interview with authors, Provo, Utah, August 17, 2013.

2. Carol S. Dweck, "The Secret to Raising Smart Kids," *Scientific American*, January 1, 2015, 1–14.

3. Steve Densley, "Set Your Course, Plan for Success" *Daily Herald*, November 14, 2014.

4. Rotella, *How Champions Think*, 104.

5.   Peterson, August 17, 2013.

6.   *Merriam-Webster's Collegiate Dictionary,* accessed November 14, 2019, https://www.merriam-webster.com/dictionary/resilience.

7.   Rotella, *How Champions Think,* 3.

8.   Irving Stone, *The Agony and the Ecstasy* (New York: Signet, 1987), 531.

9.   Dweck, "The Secret to Raising Smart Kids."

10. Dweck, "The Secret to Raising Smart Kids."

11. Included in his "America's Mission" speech, delivered at the Washington Day banquet given by the Virginia Democratic Association at Washington D.C. on February 22, 1899.

12. Julie Lythcott-Haims, in Claire Cain Miller and Jonah Engel Bromwich, "How Parents are Robbing Their Children of Adulthood," *New York Times,* March 16, 2019, https://www.nytimes.com/2019/03/16/style/snowplow-parenting-scandal.html.

13. Hara Estroff Marano, *A Nation of Wimps: The High Cost of Invasive Parenting* (New York: Broadway Books, 2008), 2.

14. "Facts and Statistics," Anxiety and Depression Association of America, National Institute of Mental Health and World Health Organization: Mental Health, https://adaa.org/about-adaa/press-room/facts-statistics.

15. 2017 National Survey on Drug Use and Health, National Institute of Mental Health, last updated February 2019, https://www.samhsa.gov/data/data-we-collect/nsduh-national-survey-drug-use-and-health.

16. Lisa Anne Jackson and Peter B. Gardner, "When the Light Goes Out," *BYU Magazine,* Spring 2017.

17. Dennis Thompson, "U.S. Youth Suicide Rate Reaches 20-Year High," Medicine.Net, June 18, 2019, https://www.medicinenet.com/script/main/art.asp?articlekey=222328.

18. Centers for Disease Control and Prevention (CDC), 2017 Youth Risk Behavior Data Summary and Trends Report 2007-2017, https://www.cdc.gov/healthyyouth/data/yrbs/pdf/trendsreport.pdf, 47.

19. "US Suicide Rates Up 33% Since 1999, Sharpest Increase among Young Adults," Daily Sabah Americas, accessed November 25, 2019, https://www.dailysabah.com/americas/2019/06/24/us-suicide-rates-up-33-since-1999-sharpest-increase-among-young-adults.

20. Rotella, *How Champions Think,* 90.

21. Mackay, "Make a Commitment to Succeed," *Daily Herald,* October 9, 2014.

Principle 3

1. Excerpt from speech, "Citizenship In A Republic" delivered at the Sorbonne in Paris, France on April 23, 1910.

2. Harvey Mackay, "Make Failure the Beginning of Greatness," *Daily Herald*, January 12, 2014.

3. Clayton M. Christensen, *How Will You Measure Your Life?* (New York: HarperCollins Publishers 2012), 152.

4. Rotella, *How Champions Think*, 185.

5. Harvey Mackay, "A Grab Bag of Humorous Morsels," *Daily Herald*, April 5, 2018.

6. J. K. Rowling, "The Fringe Benefits of Failure, and the Importance of Imagination," *Harvard Magazine*, January 8, 2013.

7. Tovia Smith, "Does Teaching Kids to Get 'Gritty' Help Them Get Ahead?" March 17, 2014, 4, NPR ED: NPR.org.

8. Napolean Hill, *Think and Grow Rich* (New York: TarcherPerisee Publishers, 2005).

9. See "Master Resilience Training (MRT) in the U.S. Army: PowerPoint & Interview," Positive Psychology Program, positivepsychologyprogram.com.

10. Levi Belnap, "I'm Thankful for failure," November 27, 2014, blog post.

11. *The Greatest Showman,* directed by Michael Gracey (California: 20th Century Fox, 2017), movie.

12. Bruno Nardini, *Michelangelo: Biography of a Genius* (Florence, Italy: Giunti Editore S.p.A., 1999), 41.

13. Sara Blakely, *Business Insider*, September 8, 2016, video.

14. Ronda Rousey, *My Fight/Your Fight* (New York: Regan Arts, 2015), 213.

15. Carroll, *Win Forever*, 177–78.

16. George Bernard Shaw, *The Doctor's Dilemma* (New York: Brentano's Publishing, 1911), lxxv, lxxxvi.

Principle 4

Epigraph: Reepicheep, *The Chronicles of Narnia: The Voyage of the Dawn Treader,* directed by Michael Apted (California: 20th Century Fox, 2010), movie.

1. Peter L. Dixon, "The Olympian" (Deerfield Illinois: Roundtable Publishing, 1984), 210.

2. Helen Adams Keller, *"Helen Keller's Journal: 1936-1937"* (New York, Doubleday, Doran and Company 1938), 60.

3. Stone, *The Agony and the Ecstasy*, 499–502.

4. "You Can Grow Your Intelligence: New Research Shows the Brain Can Be Developed Like a Muscle," National Association of Independent Schools, Winter 2008.

5. Haim Ginott, *Between Parent and Child* (New York, Three Rivers Press 2003), 169.

6. Carol S. Dweck, "The Power of Believing That You Can Improve," November 2014, TEDxNorrkoping talk.

7. Jennifer Burrows Nielson, "On Experiments and Experience," *BYU Magazine*, Summer 2015), 50.

8. Carol S. Dweck, *Mindset*, (New York: Random House, 2006), 3.

9. Kate Bassford Baker, "Please Don't Help My Kids," September 14, 2012, personal blog entry.

Principle 5

1. Ryan Freeman, "What Does 'Winning' Mean?" September 7, 2012, blog post.

2. Dan Clark, "The Four Steps on the Stairway to Heaven," BYU Devotional, September 30, 2014.

3. Stephen Palmer, "Should Living Purpose Be Easy or Hard?" Life Manifestos, December 2, 2013, 1–4.

4. Stone, *The Agony and the Ecstasy*, 512.

5. Dr. Craig Manning, *The Fearless Mind* (Springville, Utah, Cedar Fort, Inc. 2009), 80.

6. Rotella, *How Champions Think*, 170.

7. Allison Gilbert, "How to Raise a Winning Child," CNN.com, March 21, 2013.

8. Kim Lachance Shandrow, "Want Your Kid to Be Successful? Shark Tank's Barbara Corcoran Says You Should Do This," September 29, 2014, Entrepreneur.com, 2.

9. Sarah Weiser, "Making a Pointe: Teenage Boy Enjoys Non-Traditional Hobby," *Daily Herald*, March 11, 2013.

10. Francis L. Thompson, "My Rules for My Kids; Eat Your Vegetables; Don't Blame the Teacher," January 2014, theatlantic.com, 2.

11. Annabel Monaghan, *A Girl Named Digit* (New York: HMH Books for Young Readers, 2012).

Principle 6

1. Personal interview with Stephen M. R. and Jeri Covey, Provo, Utah, September 4, 2015

2. Stephen M. Covey, *The Divine Center* (Salt Lake City, Utah, Bookcraft 1982), 163.

3. Michael Robb, "Common Sense Media Census Measures Plugged-In Parents," Common Sense Media, December 6, 2016, commonsensemediaorg/plugged-in-parents-of-tweens-and-teens-2016-infographic.

4. Susan Young, "Know Who You Are," *Success Magazine*, June 2015, 43–47.

5. Bruce Feiler, "The Stories That Bind Us," *The New York Times*, March 15, 2013.

6. Charlie Campbell, "Blazing a Trail," *Time Magazine,* May 17, 2018.

7. Dr. Roy F. Baumeister, "Does High Self-Esteem Cause Better Performance, Interpersonal Success, Happiness, or Healthier Lifestyles?" *Psychological Science in the Public Interest*, 4, no. 1, May 2003.

8. Kelsey Clark, "Don't Want Materialistic Children? Avoid These Parenting Tactics," *Deseret News*, January 14, 2015.

9. Kenneth Johnson, "We All Have a Father in Whom We Can Trust," *Ensign Magazine*, May 2004.

10. Jennifer Breheny Wallace, "Why Children Need Chores," *Wall Street Journal*, March 13, 2015.

11. Covey, Stephen M. R. and Jeri, personal interview on September 4, 2015

Principle 7

Epigraph: In William Miller, *Life,* May 2, 1955.

1. Debbie Balzotti, "Zack's Shack Raises Money for Wheelchair Donations," *Daily Herald*, April 10, 2014, B1.

2. Keri Lunt Stevens, "Spanish Fork Girl Uses Own Money to Raise Money for Homeless Kids," *Daily Herald*, October 30, 2014, B1.

3. Richard Wiseman, *59 Seconds: Think a Little, Change a Lot* (London: MacMillan, 2010), 29–30.

4. Andrew Cave, "Giving to Your Church Doesn't Count: Jon Huntsman Sr. and Twitter's Biz Stone on New Philanthropy," June 6, 2014, Forbes.com.

5. Steve Densley, "Service about Self," *Daily Herald*, April 26, 2012.

6. "Max, 11-Year-Old Boy, Gives His Savings to Milwaukee Police to Honor Late Grandfather," September 17, 2013, huffingtonpost.com.

7. Mitt Romney, St. Anslem College commencement address, Goffstown, New Hampshire, May 17, 2015.

8. Anne Frank, *Anne Frank: The Diary of a Young Girl* (New York: Random House, 1952).

9. Covey, Stephen M. R. and Jeri, personal interview on September 4, 2015

10. Alice G. Walton, "Kindness Is a Key to Kids' Happiness and Popularity," January 14, 2013, thedoctorwillseeyounow.com.

11. Harvey Mackay, "Please Don't Stop Smiling," *Daily Herald,* October 18, 2019.

12. Rachel Gillett, "Research Says This Is What You Need to Teach Your Kids in Kindergarten If You Ever Want Them to Go to College or Get a Job," *Business Insider*, July 23, 2015.

13. Deborah Norville, *The Proof of Respect: Benefit from the Most Forgotten Element of Success* (Nashville, Tennessee: Thomas Nelson, 2009), 65.

14. Alex and Brett Harris, *Do Hard Things* (Colorado Springs, Colorado: Multnomah Books, 2008), 239.

15. Kimberly Hayek, "Special Needs Girl Bullied in School—Then High School Quarterback Asks Her One Simple Question," *Uplift*, October 25, 2017.

Polishing Your Family Culture of Empowerment

Epigraph: Blaine Lee, *The Power Principle.* Free Press, June 4, 1998.

1. Stone, *The Agony and the Ecstasy*, 357

2. Erica Layne, "42 Ways to Make Your Kids Feel Absolutely Loved," The Life on Purpose Movement, April 24, 2017, ericalayne.com.

3. Brené Brown, "The Power of Vulnerability," TedxHouston, June 2010.

4. Carol S. Dweck, *Mindset*, 189.

5. M. Sue Bergin, "The Imperfectly Happy Family," *BYU Magazine*, summer 2015.

6. Catherine M. Wallace, "Seven Don'ts Every Parent Should Do," *U.S. Catholic,* vol. 66, no.1, January 2001, 38-41.

7. Charles Schwab, Forbes Quotes, accessed April 11, 2019, https://www.forbes.com/quotes/1637/.

8. James Clear, "Hater & Critics: How to Deal with People Judging You," April 20, 2018, blog post.

9. Sue C. Barton, Garry L. Landreth, Theresa Kellam, and Sandra R. Blanchard, *Child Parent Relationship Manual: A 10 Session Filial Therapy Model for Parents* (New York: Routledge, July 26, 2006).

10. Mackay, "A Grab Bag of Humorous Morsels."

11. Ginott, *Between Parent and Child*, 32

12. Dweck, "The Secret to Raising Smart Kids."

13. Robin Cardon, "Joke section," *Meridian Magazine*, September 22, 2008.

14. L. R. Knost Facebook page, "Little Hearts/Gentle Parenting Resources," March 16, 2017.

15. Adam Grant, "Raising a Moral Child," *The New York Times*, April 11, 2014.

16. Larry Winget, *Grow a Pair* (New York: Gotham Books 2013), 244–45.

17. Adam Grant, "Raising a Moral Child" *The New York Times*, April 11, 2014.

18. Covey, Stephen M. R. and Jeri, personal interview on September 4, 2015.

19. Mary Clare Jalonick, "USDA Says Cost of Raising Child More Than $233K," in *Daily Herald*, January 10, 2017, A7.

20. Rosie Kaufman, "Grace for Mother and Duck," *Ensign Magazine*, August 2013.

21. *Mom of Ten,* Sanbornton, NH in response to article entitled "UVU Professors Study Put Focus on LDS Women and Depression," *Deseret News,* February 1, 2013.

You Are Michelangelo!

1. Nardini, *Michelangelo: Biography of a Genius*, 45.

2. Tad R. Callister, *The Infinite Atonement* (Salt Lake City, UT: Deseret Book, 2000), 16.

3. "Gifted Hands: The Ben Carson Story," February 7, 2009; DVD.

About the Authors

David Hagen is a retired businessman who worked in the real estate industry. Currently, he handles the business and administrative duties associated with Mindset Family Therapy.

In his spare time, he enjoys the beach, bodysurfing, reading a good book, watching college basketball (especially during March Madness), serving in his church, and checking things off his bucket list. Only twenty-eight items to go!

He needs a new right knee and works out six days a week so that hopefully he can be healthy when his twelve grandkids get married.

Amazingly, he can cook one-minute rice in fifty-two seconds, regularly challenges his grandkids to try "new and hard" things, and loves to travel.

When he first met Annabella, it was love at first sight for him; for her, it was love at six months. But he was patient!

Annabella Hagen is a former adjunct professor in the School of Social Work at Utah Valley University. She is also the owner and clinical director for Mindset Family Therapy in Provo, Utah, where she directs the efforts of eight therapists. She is a licensed clinical social worker (LCSW) and obtained her master's in social work from Brigham Young University.

Her private practice focuses on working with children, adolescents, and adults struggling with anxiety, depression, OCD, and OC spectrum disorders, as well as trauma, family issues, and parenting. Annabella enjoys serving her community by presenting on relevant topics such as parenting, anxiety, depression, and OCD.

Annabella is a member of the International OCD Foundation and a board member for the Utah Association for Play Therapy. She has been a regular presenter for both organizations.

Annabella is the author of *Emma's Worry Clouds* and *Nico the Worried Caterpillar*. She is also a frequent contributor to PsychCentral.com, other online magazines, and her business blog.

She enjoys jogging, classical music, reading, yoga, and traveling. Her favorite pastime is spending time with her twelve young grandchildren, and doing her best to be an "intentional" grandmother!

Life is good, and it's been a great journey for us so far. We can't wait to find out what the future will bring!

Made in the USA
Columbia, SC
05 November 2022

70485308R00148